*My Christmas Story Story*
Copyright ©2022 Sue Stewart, LLC

The events in this book are based on the author's recollection and may not portray actual events exactly as they occurred.

ISBN 978-1-948613-18-7
Library of Congress Control Number: 2022919497

Edited by Ruth Beach
Book Design by Stacie Gerrity

Printed in the United States of America

Sunny Day Publishing, LLC
Cuyahoga Falls, Ohio 44223
www.sunnydaypublishing.com
editor@sunnydaypublishing.com

Dedicated to my incredible
brother, Jim Moralevitz.
He guided me throughout
my life and continues to do so
from his Heavenly home.

# My Christmas Story Story

Sue Stewart

# It felt like a dream...

It was November 25, 2006. Thanksgiving weekend.

The city of Cleveland was experiencing a strange occurrence. We were enjoying an unusually warm, sunny day. Sweater weather.

I am standing near the back of a very long line of people on the street where I was born and raised. In my hand is a $5.00 admission ticket to tour a house that I had played in as a child and partied in as a teenager.

While waiting in line, my youngest grandson, Tommy, shakes me from my trance by tugging on my jacket and asking me, "Nana, do you have any gum?"

That was when I realized, this is not a dream!
Almost 5,000 people viewed *A Christmas Story* House and Museum that first weekend.
Around 50,000 people visited the house in the first year it opened.
According to Brian Jones, the House and Museum's owner, an average of 80,000 people take the tour every year.

# How did this happen?

The house I'm describing is located at 3159 West 11th Street. It is featured in the 1983 movie classic *A Christmas Story*. The house where I was born and raised is only a hop, skip, and a jump away at 3132 West 11th Street. This street is quite narrow. It is a two-way street with only one lane for vehicles to drive through. Cars are parked on both sides of this once red-bricked cobblestone road. The closely positioned houses are made of wood and most of them are two-family dwellings with a long front porch that stretches the width of the house. While standing in line, I had to laugh when I saw old and new neighbors cashing in on the whole grand opening celebration. Several residents set up large cardboard "Beer and Water for Sale" signs on their porches. They sold cans of beer and bottles of water for $1.00 each. The fact that they didn't own a vending license didn't bother these well-meaning neighbors in the least. Some neighbors were even bold enough to offer the use of their bathrooms. I did not find out how much that would cost.

People were going crazy—it was *A Christmas Story House*'s Opening Day! The residents of West 11th Street had never seen so many people on their street at one time. It felt surreal.

Little did we know that this was only the beginning. The masses would continue to gather on that street for many years to come.

As I'm standing in this line with about 100 people ahead of me, I see the driveway of my childhood home. My brother Jim lived in that house at the time and worked in *A Christmas Story* Museum. We would have parked in Jim's driveway if not for a police officer who was directing traffic, preventing any cars from driving down the street. We ended up parking in Clark Field, a ballpark located on West 11th Street, down the hill and in the opposite direction of *A Christmas Story* House. We saw two Lolly the Trolleys picking up and dropping fans off. These trolleys looked similar to the ones in San Francisco, and were continually running in a big circle, from the ball field to *A Christmas Story* House and Museum. After parking in the field, we boarded a trolley to take us back up the street and around the block. It stopped right in front of *A Christmas Story* Museum. After we stepped off, it promptly went back down to the field to load up another trolley full of fans.

This happened all day long. All weekend long.

I didn't understand why we were forced to park so far away. It seemed senseless to me, until I saw just how many people were walking around. There were hundreds of *A Christmas Story* fans excitedly waiting in expectation. Local and national television news stations sent reporters to interview the curious fans. Several cameramen were filming the large crowd.

I forgave the officer after seeing the chaos.

A crowd gathered in the intersection between the house and the museum. The anticipation in the air was palpable while everyone waited to see the stars of the movie.

Those who lived around the House had a hard time getting to their driveways. They had to show their driver's license to the cop so he could check their address.

As I waited in line for nearly an hour, I saw Lolly the Trolley ferrying a continuous stream of people, dropping around 20 people off in front of the museum every 10 minutes or so.

I noticed that my friend Teddy was standing in the doorway to the Rowley Inn, his beer garden across the street. Back in the day, neighborhood bars were called "beer gardens."

I cheerfully yelled out across the noisy street, "Hey Teddy, how is business today?"

"Oh Susie, business is fantastic today!" he yelled back. "My place is packed!" I told Teddy that he would need to expand his place to accommodate the throngs of fans who would be stopping by his conveniently located bar after visiting the House.

After about an hour, the actors filed out of the House to gather on the front porch. They smiled and waved. The crowd went wild!

It was strange to see them all grown up. After all, it was 23 years since the movie was made. There they were: Ian Petrella (Randy), Yano Anaya (Grover Dill), Zack Ward (Scut Farkus), and Scott Schwartz (Flick). Tedde Moore (Miss Shields) was also on the front porch with them. Unfortunately, the three main actors were unable to be there. Melinda Dillon (Mother Parker) lived in France at the time, Darren McGavin (The Old Man) was in poor health, and Peter Billingsley (Ralphie Parker) had prior commitments. That did not deter the excited crowd of *A Christmas Story* fans.

Brian Jones, the owner of *A Christmas Story* House and Museum, proudly directed the festivities. Since this was the actual porch where the "FRAGILE" Leg Lamp crate was delivered in the movie, a parody was arranged depicting the scene. A large wooden crate stamped with "FRAGILE" was rolled up to Brian. Brian excitedly opened it and pulled out a large Leg Lamp. The crowd erupted in cheers!

On that day, the phenomenon started. It has not stopped.

Today, movie-making is pretty common in and around Cleveland, Ohio. Many of them were blockbuster movies like *Major League, Air Force One, The Avengers,* and *Captain America: The Winter Soldier.* Because of television and social media, we know exactly what day, the location, and who will be filming what in order for crowds to gather and catch a glimpse of the action. There's a good chance of being a part of the movie, as they always need extras.

The Best Picture Oscar-winning movie of 1978, *The Deer Hunter,* was filmed in the Tremont area. Because of the success of that movie, when movie crews returned there in 1983, it was big news. If you asked anyone in Northeastern Ohio today about the filming of *A Christmas Story,* I'm sure they would have a story or two about knowing a friend, family member, neighbor, friend of a friend, family member of a neighbor, etc., who were involved in some way with the making of that famous movie.

We all have our stories—I would like to tell you a few that you never knew.

*A Christmas Story* House and Museum is not your average holiday-themed attraction. Throughout the year, there is always something new and exciting going on in and around Cleveland that is associated with the movie, held with the sole purpose of raising money for charity.

I have personally witnessed dedicated enthusiasts of *A Christmas Story* wait in long lines just to tour *A Christmas Story* House and Museum throughout the year.

*A Christmas Story* mania has had a far-reaching impact. The visitor's log at the museum is filled with names and addresses from as far as Australia and Japan. Many of these fans have commented about their family tradition of watching the movie every Christmas. Some have saved for years to make the trek just to cross this experience off their bucket list. Many simply state their joy of just being where it all originated.

This is an informative account of what happened when Hollywood came to my tiny neighborhood to film what we thought would be just another Christmas movie…

Nothing would be the same for my old neighborhood ever again.

Bob Clark & Darren McGavin discussing movie production

# Filming *A Christmas Story*

For those of you who aren't familiar with *A Christmas Story*—where have you been? I know you're out there. Here's a synopsis, just for you:

The 1983 movie was adapted from several stories of author Jean Shepherd's childhood from his book, *In God We Trust, All Others Pay Cash*. Appropriately, Mr. Shepherd is also the narrator of this film, giving voice to the adult Ralphie Parker.

A 10-year-old boy named Ralphie Parker wants what he considers the greatest gift he could ever receive for Christmas—a Red Ryder Range Model Air Rifle. His parents, his teacher, and even Santa try to dissuade him. They all keep telling him, "you'll shoot your eye out."

Ralphie's dad, the "Old Man," is distraught about the many upsets in his life. He's having a hard time with the neighbors' many noisy and wild hounds. He's fighting a losing battle with an unpredictable furnace. He gets a flat tire, resulting in one of the most comical scenes in this movie—as Ralphie is helping his dad fix the flat, he accidentally hits the hubcap holding all the nuts and bolts. They fly everywhere in the snow, and Dad hears Ralphie blurt out the famous line, "Oh fuuuuuuuudge" (only that's not the word he chooses). Consequently, when they return home, Ralphie ends up with a bar of soap in his mouth.

The Old Man's life brightens when he wins a "Major Award' that turns out to be a lamp shaped like a woman's leg wearing a fishnet stocking. He's elated but his wife dislikes it. "The Battle of the Lamp" results in Mrs.

Parker accidentally breaking the light fixture.

Throughout the movie, Ralphie and his friends are tormented by the neighborhood bully, Scut Farkus, and his sidekick, Grover Dill. Ralphie is driven to his breaking point and fights back.

Towards the end of the movie, Ralphie and his family are opening presents on Christmas morning. He is disappointed—no air rifle. He thinks, "no one was listening, no one understands." Well, his dad listened. He understood. Dad nods toward the corner where, lo and behold, there is a hidden present—the beloved air rifle!

At the end of the film, Ralphie is lying in his bed with the rifle by his side. He smiles with the thought that this was indeed the best present he had ever received or would ever receive.
The End.

Jean Shepherd based Ralphie on himself. Ralphie's little brother Randy was named after Jean's real-life brother. Their last name, Parker, is Jean's middle name. Mr. Shepherd broadcast these same stories on his radio show in the 1950s. Bob Clark loved to listen to this radio show. As he tells it, he was driving to a date's house when he started listening to Jean Shepherd's radio show and ended up driving around for nearly an hour, listening to the program until it was over. Needless to say, Bob Clark's date was not happy, but he knew that he wanted to make a movie out of those stories. Later, he became good friends with Jean Shepherd and they felt that these combined stories would be a big hit as a movie. Bob Clark's official title for the movie was Director, Co-Writer & Co-Producer.

Before applying his talents to creating *A Christmas Story*, he had just written and directed a big hit of a movie called *Porky's*. That movie was very popular and afforded him the luxury of looking for a production company that would assist him in the making of a Christmas movie. Because *Porky's* was such a big hit, MGM wanted Bob Clark to direct *Porky's II*. Now he had leverage, and he used it. He said he would do a *Porky's II*, but only after he was done with *A Christmas Story*. He was true to his word.

While in Canada, Bob Clark teamed up with Christmas Tree Productions, a film company based in Toronto. MGM studio gave them approximately $2 million to make the movie. According to Caseen Gaines' 2013 book about this film, he waived his director's fee and provided $150,000 of his own money.

Bob Clark sent location scouts to look at over 20 cities, trying to find the perfect neighborhood. In the movie, the Parkers lived in Indiana, the home state of Jean Shepherd. One of Bob's main objectives for the movie was to film the Santa scene in a real department store. The Cleveland Historical website states that he sent 100 letters out to department stores across the country, asking if they would be willing to allow him to film the Santa scene in their store. Thankfully, the incredibly beautiful Higbee's Department Store, which was located in the heart of downtown Cleveland, was the only store that responded with a resounding "Yes!"

In a *Cleveland Plain Dealer* newspaper article from 2006, Mr. Bruce Campbell, Higbee's President of the Department of Administration at that time, stated that he welcomed the publicity. He offered 1,000 workers to feed the crew, style the performers' hair, build sets, and serve as extras. Mr. Campbell also stated that "much to my amazement," he persuaded Bob Clark to soften the script's language. Bob agreed to it and filming in the store began. Jean Shepherd made up gibberish words to replace the curse words, making the movie more comical. That cursing stipulation helped the movie become a PG-rated family classic.

Although it was January, 1983 and the Christmas season was over, Higbee's Department Store allowed the set decorators to fill the large display windows with many of their old-fashioned toys from the 1930s. The city of Cleveland was also willing to keep the Christmas trees and street lighting displays up until after the crew finished filming. The production company supplied additional Christmas lights to string across the streets and to adorn the office buildings. My husband, Bob, and I went for a ride with our children to downtown Cleveland to witness the Christmas lights in the middle of January for ourselves. Our city looked great in the movie—but even better in reality!

Bob Clark decided that since he'd be filming the Santa scene in the Higbee's store in Cleveland, he wanted to film other scenes in Cleveland. He remembered seeing our Tremont area from the movie *The Deer Hunter*, and loved the look of the neighborhood with its 1930 Depression-style houses. Many fans are surprised to learn that the beautiful wedding reception scene in *The Deer Hunter* was filmed in Lemko Hall, which is right down the street from *A Christmas Story* House.

A location scout was driving down Rowley Avenue when he spotted the house at 3159 West 11th Street, situated right at the end of this street. The area had many advantages, one of them being that it was at a 3-way intersection. That would make it easier for large semi-trucks to move around and park, and for cameras and equipment to be set up. He'd found the spot!

This house had a decent-sized yard and a big picture window. It also helped that both the backyard of *A Christmas Story* House and that of the neighboring house (the Bumpuses') looked out over the valley of the steel mills. There were no neighbors behind the houses to distract from the scenes, only the mills. In fact, the opening scene of the movie is of our mountainous steel mills in all their smoking glory. Jean Shepherd grew up in an industrial town and wanted the mills in the movie. Originally, the opening scene had Ralphie and his buddies, Flick and Schwartz, running across a steelyard with a slag heap in the foreground, with little brother Randy trailing behind. That scene ended up on the cutting room floor.

Bob Clark immediately liked the photos of the house and neighborhood. The stars must have been in alignment for Bob Clark because the soon-to-be Parker house and the Bumpus house were both vacant at that time—perfect for filming without interruptions or extra expenses. There really wasn't much traffic on that street either. The only cars driving by were those of the residents, friends, and the customers for the Rowley Inn bar.

Since they were filming so many scenes in Cleveland, the location scouts were on the lookout for a 1939-type, red-brick grade school. They wanted the school to be in a typical neighborhood, with no high-rises in the background. They also needed a large school playground for all their trucks and equipment. They didn't find that particular school in Cleveland, so they filmed the school scenes at Victoria School in St. Catharines, Ontario, Canada. The fact that Canada, unlike Cleveland, had a lot of real snow all over the schoolyard that year also helped a lot.

I went to kindergarten in just such a red-brick school as they were looking for. It was called Buhrer School, located on Buhrer Avenue, right around the corner and two blocks down the street from the House. Unfortunately, it was just a memory in 1983 because in the 1960s, this school and many houses in our neighborhood were demolished to pave the way for Interstate 71. If only it weren't torn down, it would have been perfect. On the bright side, thanks to Victoria School, we were able to share this movie with Canada.

# Darren McGavin is in My Driveway!

I cannot help but brag about my beloved brother Jim. He played a pivotal role in bringing the movie to our neighborhood by arranging a meeting between the production company and the owner of 3159 West 11th St., the vacant house that was destined for the silver screen.

Jim was living in our family's home in January, 1983. He loved to visit with his friends at the corner bar, the Rowley Inn. It was very convenient to walk there, as it was less than 20 feet away from his home. Jim just happened to be in the Rowley Inn when, as he tells it, "it was 3:15 in the afternoon, just another regular day, when a beautiful casting director by the name of Julie Matthews walked into the bar. She pointed to that house across the street and asked if anyone knew who owned it." Well, of course, Jim knew who owned that house. He was nicknamed "The Mayor of West 11th Street" for a reason—Jim knew everyone in that neighborhood. I'm telling you, he always seemed to be in the right place at the right time. Jim walked up to Julie and said, "Yes, I know who owns that house. It's my buddy, John."

Jim asked Julie to sit down and have a drink because John would be coming in momentarily. John always stopped by the Rowley Inn for a "cold one" right after work. Just as Jim predicted, John arrived soon after and was introduced to Julie.

Within a week, production crews for the movie appeared. When Darren McGavin, Melinda Dillon, and Peter Billingsley came to town to begin filming, we were star-struck. Hollywood had arrived!

My little neighborhood was filled with anticipation and excitement as those huge semi-trucks rolled down our little street. These semis stayed long enough to offload the multitude of production materials, much of which were several shapes and sizes of cameras and lighting equipment. They were stored inside the vacant house, as only the outside was being filmed.

These streets are narrow with very tight parking spaces between the driveways, especially for the large equipment trucks. Bob Clark needed a place to set up makeup and wardrobe. One of the apartments above Rowley Inn was vacant at the time, so the Christmas Tree Films company set up shop for a month. Now the actors had a place to change clothes and take a break. Among the essentials, a barbershop was set up in one of the vacant bedrooms. There was an office and a snack area set up in the living room. Some of the impromptu photographs in this book of Peter and the other young actors were taken by Jim from the vantage point of leaning out of the apartment's upstairs windows.

Several neighbors were asked if they would rent out their driveways to make room for all the vehicles associated with the movie. Always accommodating, Jim was one of the first to allow them to park in his driveway. The compensation was small, but he didn't mind. He had no idea what would be parked there. Jim parked his own car a few blocks away, down the hill, near Clark Field. By the time he walked up the hill and back to his house, there was a medium-sized dressing trailer parked in his driveway. He was told that Darren McGavin would be using this dressing trailer during production. Jim was delighted! There were several limousines on standby to transport the actors to and from their hotels. Jim was permitted to use a limousine to buy his groceries when he needed to do his weekly shopping.

I remember the day when Jim called me on the phone. He was so excited. He was laughing when he said to me, "Susie, Darren McGavin's dressing trailer is in my driveway!" Now, Jim knew that I liked Darren's old tele-

Jim Moralevitz & Darren McGavin

vision show *The Night Stalker*. I, of course, thought it was another outlandish "Jimmy joke" that he was known for. I teasingly asked Jim if Darren (who played reporter Carl Kolchak) was looking for a vampire like he did in his TV series. Not this time. He was about to portray the famous "Old Man Parker."

For Jim—and for Darren—the fun was just beginning. It was the start of a wonderful friendship. They had a similar sense of humor and outlook on life. They talked and laughed for hours. Nothing was off-limits with them.

Darren and his wife, Kathie, stayed at the former Stouffer's Hotel (now the Renaissance Hotel) in downtown Cleveland, along with the other stars of the film. Darren must have been a very early riser because before Jim even walked out the front door of his house each morning, Darren was already in his trailer, getting ready for work. All the hair and makeup people would be fussing around Mr. McGavin. He would see Jim walking past his window and yell out, "good morning Jim!" And Jim would say, "good morning Darren!" They worked long hours. Darren had his lines to memorize and parts to play. Jim was busy helping the crew set up/take down equipment, chaperoning the young actors, and assisting Bob Clark with production duties. That happened nearly every day for almost a month.

Darren calling his wife

Often, after the day's film[...] [...] [...] [...]e workers and
actors, including Jim and Dar[...] [...]ey Inn for dinner and to relax. Our family f[...] [...] and prepared
hearty meat and potato dishe[...] [...]. With the film
crew continually stopping by, [...] [...]. He said the
workers never complained abo[...] [...]e meals, they
just kept coming back for mor[...]

Back then, there was a hug[...] [...]he corner of
the bar. Every night he stoppe[...] [...]booth, leave
the door open, and call his w[...] [...] of Darren
in this booth with the door [...] [...]swered the
phone, he'd say, "Hi Honey, sh[...] [...]at the bar
with my good friend Jim, and [...] [...]old ones."
Darren never closed the telep[...] [...]ne else at
the bar could hear every word [...] [...]y.

Once in a while, they woul[...] [...]hat happened, they would walk a few [...] [...]use and
discuss anything and everything. Darren always had a limo ride back to
the hotel. Jim was well aware of how fortunate he was to have a bona fide
Hollywood star right in his own front yard. Jim told me he was on cloud
nine the whole time.

During one rehearsal of the Swede scene, Bob Clark was busy directing, so Jim filled in for him and read Swede's lines. This scene takes place outside the house and across the street, when The Old Man is directing Mrs. Parker on centering the Leg Lamp in the window. The original script called for The Old Man saying, "Move it a little to the left, okay!" and "You oughta see it from here!" Darren ad-libbed the whole conversation with Swede.

During rehearsal, Jim watched as Darren stood up, keeping one hand behind his back holding his notepad. If he forgot a line, he'd whip the notepad out from behind him, mumble the words and then say "ok, got it." Then he'd recite the line from memory. Inside this book are copies of Darren's actual notes, written on an 8 ½ x 11 legal pad, that he composed for this scene with Swede. He thought up additional lines to say, and used these notes to practice these lines with Jim. Over the years, Darren's original notepad was becoming discolored and, well, fragile. To keep his handwritten notes preserved, I donated them to *A Christmas Story* Museum where they are appropriately secured inside a glass case, located in the same room where Jim worked for years.

The next time you watch that scene, look at Darren's notes in this book—they are almost word for word what ended up in the movie. An interesting fact about this scene—Bob Clark did not have a southern accent, but provided one for his character, Swede. He never explained why he chose a southern accent over a Swedish one, or any accent at all.

Darren loved to make up words. During one of his conversations with Jim, Darren said the word "nottafinga." Jim asked him what that word meant and Darren said: "I don't know. I just made it up. You have the privilege of being the first person to ever hear it."

Darren used "nottafinga" in the scene where Mrs. Parker accidentally breaks the lamp and The Old Man is frantic to put it back together again. He says he will glue it. Mrs. Parker says that there isn't any glue in the house.

Darren (laughing) & Bob Clark as Swede

He is getting angrier by the minute.

The narration for that scene: "The Old Man stood quivering with fury, staring as he tried to come up with a real crusher. All he could get out was: nottafinga!"

Darren created another new word heard in the film. He made up his own curse words to get the point across. In the scene where he is fighting with the furnace, you can hear him say, "dollywop!" Darren took his work very seriously. He would recite his movie lines first thing in the morning, after breakfast. He would say them over and over until he was satisfied with them. Jim got a kick out of watching the great actor practice his craft.

(Darren wasn't the only wordsmith: during an interview in 2003, Bob Clark said that it was his idea to turn "FRAGILE" into "Fra-GEE-lay.")

Jim felt privileged to call Darren his friend. They remained friends up until Darren's death on February 25, 2006. Since Jim's passing, I would like to think that they are sharing a few cold ones up in heaven.

Darren & Bob Clark as Swede looking at the leg lamp in the window

Because the movie was a Christmas movie, there needed to be a lot of snow. Director Bob Clark had worked out his schedule to start filming the movie in January. A child of the south, Bob Clark assumed that it always snowed in Cleveland in January. As it turned out, although we had freezing temperatures, there was very little snowfall accumulation throughout the month of January in 1983. Because of that, the crews had to work hard to create their own winter wonderland. The special effects team worked tirelessly, day and night, spraying water all over trees and houses to make icicles. Jim was hired as a crew assistant. I don't believe they paid very much, but he didn't mind. To him, the whole experience was priceless. He started working alongside crew members every day, doing anything he could to help out. Bob Clark took a liking to Jim. Jim told Bob that he watched the early morning news and weather on television every day. It became a ritual—Bob would ask Jim, "is it going to snow today?" Jim's answer was almost al-

BOB CLARK'S CAMEO BENCH

In memory of Bob Clark, Director of "A Christmas Story"
AUGUST 5, 1939 – APRIL 4, 2007

Darren McGavin as Old Man Parker giving directions

Melinda Dillon as Mother Parker adjusting the lamp

Peter Billingsley as Ralphie & Ian Petrella as Randy

Old Man Parker & the Bumpus hounds

**Associated**   **LEGAL RULED PAD**          P3-C811WP

S :   HEY, PARKER THAT'S SOME LAMP....——

OM :   DON+ BOTHER ME SWEDE.....CAN'T YOU SEE I'M BUSY?..

S :   +HAT SURE IS A LAMP...

OM. (IRRITATED)   IT'S A MAJOR AWARD........

S:   DAMN, LOOKS LIKE A LAMP TO ME.....

OM:   IT IS ALAMP BUT IT'S A MAJOR AWARD.........
                                              I WON IT!

S:   WELL I SWAN... A MAJOL AWARD, NEVER
        SEEN ONE OF THEM THINGS.....—

OM:   YEP....—A—M

S:   DAMN, IT SURE IS A DOOZY.

MOVE - TO LEFT- MORE ...... EASY -
Boy YOU SHOULD SEE IT FROM OUT HERE!

S:   HEY PARKER, WHAT IS THAT.....

O:M:   DON'T BOTHER ME SWEDE, CAN'T YOU SEE IM BUSY?

S:   WHAT IS IT?

OM (WITH PRIDE)   A MAJOR AWARD -

S.   DAMN, I WOULDN'T HAVE KNOWED IT... LOOKS LIKE A LAMP

OM:   IT IS A LAMP STUPID, BUT IT'S A MAJOR AWARD
                                  I WON IT

S   DAMN, HELL YOU SAY ·· YOU WON?

OM:   ~~TAKES TALENT SWEDE~~.

OM:   MIND POWER, SWEDE... ~Ref/~

S:   WELL, DAMN, IT SURE IS A DOOZY -

OM)   A LITTLE TO THE RIT... THERE!

A different view of the opening scene of *A Christmas Story* movie

ways "no." Bob was getting worried, but Jim had an idea.

How do you get snow when it's not snowing? Jim was very familiar with that dilemma. He was a co-founder and former tour director for the High-Rise Ski Club, where he accompanied skiers to ski resorts all over the world. He told Bob about snow-making machines. Bob asked, "Do you really need snow-making machines in Northern Ohio?"

Jim said, "Yes, and I know some people at a nearby ski resort." That same day, Jim convinced his friends at the Brandywine Ski Resort to lend four of their snow-making machines for the film. In addition to the snow-making machines, the crew also made their own snow from a mixture of fire-fighting foam and Styrofoam. They worked tirelessly to create a winter wonderland. They set up one of the snow machines in the backyard of the House, and the other three were situated on the streets surrounding the House.

Problem solved, right? Well, at least that part of the problem was solved…

The whole area surrounding the House needed to be under a blanket of snow. That included all the nearby houses. Jim and some of the crewmembers went knocking on doors throughout the neighborhood. They asked the tenants for signed permissions to have snow blown onto their houses at all hours of the day and night with very noisy snow blowers.

Our cousin John lived on the corner lot, located directly across from the House. Although John had a front-row seat during the filming, he didn't venture out of his house very much in the winter, even if there were cameras and movie stars around. He kept to himself. His house would be in many scenes. It was crucial he said yes. John might have only agreed because it was Jim who asked. John allowed the snow machines to cover his house and yard—after all, his flowers and plants were dormant during the winter months. John's house would later become *A Christmas Story* Museum.

Making snow

At first, a lot of neighbors turned the workers down. They were excited that a movie was being made, sure, but they were already inconvenienced by the lack of parking and the heavy traffic. One woman told Jim that her husband had to get up very early in the morning and he needed a peaceful sleep, which would be impossible with the snow-making machines roaring all night. One day, while trying to convince a woman to allow her house to be doused in snow, Jim saw a young boy sitting on the couch. Jim asked her, "Is that little boy your son? Would he like to be an extra in the movie?" It worked.

Snow on the Bumpus House

It worked for every snow-averse homeowner on the street.

There were around eight to ten children and several adults who got to play extras in the movie just for agreeing to have snow blown on their houses all through the night.

While filming, there was another complication. One of the neighbors had his brand new 1983 Buick parked in his driveway, which was near the House. This car was beautiful, and he did not want to park it down the street, out of his sight.

The Bumpus House

Bob Clark was directing a scene where the boys were walking home from school. They would be filmed walking right past this man's house.

Now, everyone knows that a 1983 Buick does not belong in a 1939 movie. After some time, this guy was fi-

Period cars parked next to what is now *A Christmas Story* gift shop

nancially persuaded to remove it from his driveway, and filming commenced.

One day, my husband, Bob, our son Tim, and I stopped by to watch Jim at work and try to get a glimpse of the stars. Jim asked Bob Clark if we could stay and watch them work. Bob looked at us, looked at our adorable four-year-old son, Tim, and said: 'Okay, as long as they're quiet'. He certainly did not want a crying toddler interrupting the filming. I didn't know it at the time, but we ended up having the honor of observing Bob Clark directing Ralphie's dream sequence: Black Bart and his Marauders scene. In this scene, Black Bart and his bandits are on the monkey bars in the Parkers' backyard. Ralphie is imagining himself as a cowboy, boldly aiming his treasured Red Ryder Range Model Air Rifle gun through the back window of the house while his family helplessly cowers under the kitchen table. He manages to shoot all the bandits and save the day, thanks to his Red Ryder BB gun.

In this dream scene, there are monkey bars and a small trampoline in the backyard for Black Bart and his Marauders. The bars were later removed and an archway/trellis was put up in that same backyard for the Ralphie Shoots His Eye Out scene.

Black Bart, by the way, was a real guy—an outlaw who lived in the 1800s and was noted for leaving poetic messages after two of his robberies. It seems poetic that his life of infamy turned him into a character in *A Christmas Story*.

The atmosphere on-set was lively and joyful. I know I was certainly joyful just observing. The stuntmen playing the Marauders had a lot of fun that day. We could tell that they really enjoyed their work. They kept trying different poses on the monkey bars as Ralphie shot them. They used a lot of ropes, pulleys, and cable rigs to protect themselves when they were upside down on the monkey bars or falling off the shed. That took a lot of time to set up. Safety for the men came first, so many precautionary measures had to be taken. They also had to be careful not to get the riggings on camera.

Something to look for in the movie—Ralphie fires the gun three times, but four of the Marauders are seen lying in a pile with Xs on their eyes.

During the Black Bart fantasy scene, we see Ralphie the cowboy spitting tobacco juice. For reasons unknown, a crew member gave Peter real chewing tobacco. Not a good idea. Peter grew ill. His mouth was burning and he had an upset stomach. Afterward, Peter was only allowed to chew and spit ground raisins.

Bob and I captured many one-of-a-kind pictures that day. Thanks to Jim, we could watch the action as long as we were quiet. We met Dwayne McLean, who played Black Bart. Dwayne was originally hired as a stunt coordinator. He said he had no idea that he would be playing a role. At the last minute, Bob Clark told Dwayne, "go to

Black Bart's Marauders

wardrobe and put on the striped shirt and black pants." He did. They fit. Simple as that.

Dwayne used a trampoline to jump over the fence and up onto the horse. Jim and Dwayne joked around a lot that day. Spirits were high. During production, Jim situated us in the Bumpuses' side yard, which had a clear view of the Parkers' backyard. We watched for several hours with quiet excitement. I noticed that Black Bart's magnificent tan horse was very well behaved. He was not at all nervous with the bright lights and film crew around. I donated a copy of a picture I took of this beautiful horse to the *Christmas Story* Museum when it first opened. At that time, it was the only picture of him that the Museum had. It still might be.

Black Bart's Horse

Bob Clark, Darren McGavin, Melinda Dillon, & film crew

Melinda Dillon, Darren McGavin, Bob Clark, & film crew

CHRISTMAS TREE FILMS INC      CALL SHEET      CONTACT PRODUCTION OFFICE 216 771-8010

"A CHRISTMAS STORY"

PRODUCERS: RENE DUPONT / BOB CLARK     DAY 11   DATE WEDNESDAY JANUARY 26 '83
DIRECTOR: BOB CLARK      LOCATION   3159 W 11TH ST
PRODUCTION MANAGER: MARILYN STONEHOUSE     241-8951

**10/6**

UNIT CALL   11:00 AM DEPART STOUFFERS

| | ARTISTE | CHARACTER | P/U | | M/U / HAIR | SET CALL |
|---|---|---|---|---|---|---|
| 2 | MS MELINDA DILLON | MUTHA | 12:00N | 1026 | 12:15 N | 1:00 PM |
| 1 | MR DARREN McGAVIN | OLD MAN | | 1143 | S/B HOTEL FROM 12:00N | |
| 3 | MASTER BILLINGSLEY | RALPHIE | 11:15 AM | 922 | 11:30 AM | 12:00 N |
| 4 | MASTER PETRELLA | RANDY | | 949 | S/B HOTEL FROM 12:00N | |
| 5 | MASTER SCHWARTZ | FLICK | | 1408 | S/B HOTEL FROM 12:00N | |
| 6 | MASTER ROBB | SCHWARTZ | | 1460 | S/B HOTEL FROM 12:00N | |
| 11 | MR JIM HUNTER | FREIGHTMAN | 5:30 PM | 562 | 5:45 PM | 6:15 PM |
| | MS LARSEN & MR YOUNG | STAND-INS | | | | 12:00 N |
| A | | 2 FREIGHTMEN | | | 5:30 PM | 6:00 PM |
| B | | STREET CROWD (10) | | | | TBA |

| SETS | | SCENE NOS | CAST | D/N | PAGES |
|---|---|---|---|---|---|
| INT/EXT BEDROOM - BACKYARD | RALPH'S P.O.V OF ICY WONDERLAND | 72 pt | 3 | D | 1/8 |
| EXT BACKYARD ('ICELAND) | RALPHIE SHOOTS HIMSELF | 74 pt | 2, 3 | D | 1 4/8 |

IF NOT SUNNY PREPARE FOR THE FOLLOWING DAYLIGHT SCENES:

| SETS | | SCENE NOS | CAST | D/N | PAGES |
|---|---|---|---|---|---|
| EXT FRONT DOOR (FANTASY) | RAY CHARLES TAP-TAPS HOME | 45 | 2, 3 | D | 2/8 |
| EXT RALPH'S HOUSE | RALPH RECEIVES DECODER | 51 | 3, 4, 6 | D | 1 1/8 |
| EXT RALPH'S HOUSE | OFF TO SCHOOL | 57 | 1, 2, 3, 4, 5, A | D | 4/8 |

IF SOLAR ECLIPSE OR OTHER LIGHT-ROBBING PHENOMENON LIKE NIGHTFALL:

| SETS | | SCENE NOS | CAST | D/N | PAGES |
|---|---|---|---|---|---|
| EXT RALPH'S HOUSE (UNSCRIPTED) | DELIVERING BOOBY (LEGGY) PRIZE | A30 | 1, 2, 3, 4, 11, A, B | N | - |
| EXT RALPH'S HOUSE | PLAYING SANTA | 69 | 1, 2 | N | 2/8 |
| EXT RALPH'S HOUSE | REPAIRING LAMP / JUNKING IT | 54, 56 | 1 | N | 5/8 |

TRANSPORTATION: CREW BUS DEPART HOTEL AT 11:00 AM . ARTIST P/U'S AS PER ABOVE.
     S/B VELOCEPE FOR MR CLARK AT 11:00 AM
     MOTORHOMES & PRODUCTION TRUCKS READY ON LOCATION AT 11:00 AM
     S/B LUNCH SHUTTLE TO ST MICHAELS AT 3:00 - 5:00 PM
     SCISSOR LIFT W/ KEY ON LOCATION

PROPS: B.B. GUN (PRACTICAL); TARGET; AMMO; WHITE CANE; MAIL INCL RALPH'S PKG. (DBLS TO BE
     OPENED; DECODER PIN; MEMBERSHIP CARD W/ INSCRIPTION; SCHOOL BOOKS; LEG CARTON
     DOLLEY; BROKEN GLASSES; MAILBOX; LAMP BROKEN & REPAIRED

PICTURE VEHICLES: S/B 6 CARS ON WILL NOTIFY FROM 11:00 AM

EFX: BACKYARD ICELAND; CHIMNEY SMOKE; SNOW; WIND; GUN PRACTICAL;

MAKE-UP: B.B. INJURY.

WARDROBE: RALPH'S FANTASY ATTIRE INCL SHADES

ANIMALS: BUMPUS DOGS ATTACK SC 57 S/B AT HOTEL FOR NOTIFICATION FROM 11:00 AM

CATERING: LUNCH FOR 110 AT ST MICHAELS AT 4:00 PM

TUTORING: CLASSES IN ROOM 512 AT 9:00 AM

WEATHER FORECAST: FLURRIES OVERNIGHT LOW 17°-22°. WEDNESDAY INTERMITTENT CLOUD & SUN
     WITH OCCASSIONAL FLURRIES HIGH 24°-29°F. NIGHTIME LOWS 7°-12°F

ADVANCE SCHEDULE

VARIOUS SCENES SHOOTING SOMEWHERE EAST OF A LINE RUNNING THROUGH
GREAT SLAVE LAKE & LITTLE ROCK ARKANSAS

CHRISTMAS TREE FILMS INC      CALL SHEET      CONTACT PRODUCTION OFFICE 216 771·8010
"A CHRISTMAS STORY"

PRODUCERS: RENE DUPONT / BOB CLARK     DAY 12     DATE THURSDAY JAN· 27 1983
DIRECTOR: BOB CLARK     LOCATION A 3159 W 11TH ST   621-6541
PRODUCTION MANAGER: MARILYN STONEHOUSE     A) CLARK ST BRIDGE
     UNIT CALL 9:00 AM DEPART     B 1970 SCRANTON AVE
     STOUFFERS

| | ARTISTE | CHARACTER | P/U | M/U / HAIR | SET CALL |
|---|---|---|---|---|---|
| 2 | MS MELINDA DILLON | MOTHER | S/B HOTEL FROM 12:00 N | | |
| 1 | MR DARREN McGAVIN | OLD MAN | S/B HOTEL FROM 12:00 N | | |
| 3 | MASTER BILLINGSLEY | RALPH | 11:15 AM | 11:30 AM | 12:00 N |
| 4 | MASTER PETRELLA | RANDY | 11:15 AM | 11:30 AM | 12:00 N |
| 5 | MASTER SCHWARTZ | FLICK | 9:00 AM | 9:15 AM | 9:45 AM |
| 6 | MASTER ROBB | SCHWARTZ · | 9:00 AM | 9:15 AM | 9:45 AM |
| 8 | MASTER ANAYA | DILL | NOT CALLED | | |
| 10 | MASTER WARD | FARKAS | NOT CALLED | | |
| | MR DALE YOUNG | *for* OLD MAN | | | 12:00 N |
| 2A | MS KAREN LARSON | *for* MOTHER | | | 12:00 N |
| B | | TRAM DRIVER | | 2:00 PM | 2:30 PM |
| A | | CROWD (6) | | 9:15 AM | 9:45 AM |
| 4A | MASTER BLUMENTHAL | DBL RANDY | | | TBA |

| SETS | SCENE NOS | CAST | D/N | PAGES | LOCATION |
|---|---|---|---|---|---|
| EXT STEEL MILLS <br> FLICK + SCHWARTZ RUNNING | 1 | 5, 6, | D | 5/8 | A |
| EXT STEEL MILLS / HOUSE <br> RALPH + RANDY JOIN IN | 2 pt | 3, 4, 5, 6, A | D | 1/8 | A |
| EXT· RALPH'S DOMICILE <br> DECODER ARRIVES IN MAIL | 51 pt | 3, 4, 6, A | D | 1 1/8 | A |
| EXT· RALPH'S HOUSE <br> OFF TO SCHOOL | 12 pt | 3, 4, 5, A | D | 1 1/8 | A |
| EXT SCHWARTZ'S HOUSE <br> ARM PUNCH RITUAL | 13 | 3, 4, 5, 6, A | D | 1 3/8 | A |
| EXT RALPH'S HOUSE <br> OFF TO SCHOOL AGAIN | 57 | 1, 3, 4 | D | 4 8 | A |
| EXT STEEL MILL <br> BOARDING THE TRAM | 3 | 3, 4, 5, 6, B | D | 2/8 | B |
| EXT OLDSMOBILE <br> CHANGING FLAT | 41 COMP, 42 COMP | 1, 2, 3, 4, 2A, 4A | N | 3 | B |

· * SEE ADVANCE SCHEDULE FOR POSSIBLE SUBSTITUTIONS AND / OR TARGET OF OPPORTUNITY

TRANSPORTATION CREW BUS DEPART HOTEL AT 9:00 AM· S/B FOR LOCATION MOVES· ARTIST P/U'S AS ABOVE
     MOTORHOMES · PRODUCTION TRUCKS S/B AT 9:00 AM TO MOVE AS DIRECTED LOC A → LOC A
     TRAM TO LOC B AT 2:00 PM
     SCISSOR LIFTS ON LOC B AT 5:00 PM (2 LIFTS )
     S/B CAR FOR MR· CLARK AT HOTEL AT 9:00 AM

PROPS: SCHOOL BOOKS; MAIL INCL DBLS OF PKG W/ DECODER PIN + MEMBERSHIP CARD; SPARE TIRE ; JACK
     WHEEL NUTS W/ SPARES ( FLAT TIRE); CONTINUITY TREE + ROPES, WHEEL WRENCH; HUB CAP );
     RIGGED FLASHLIGHT; MAIL BOX

PICTURE VEHICLES · TRAM CAR 2:00 PM LOC B; 6 CARS LOC A 9:30 AM ; S/B 3 TRUCKS LOC B WILL NOT
     OLDSMOBILE LOC A 9:00 AM + LOC· B
EFX ACRID SMOKE ; SNOW ; WIND ; BLACK SMOKE WHITE SMOKE

CAMERA LONG ZOOM LENS SCS 1, 2 , HIGH SPEED CAMERA SC· 41, 42

DOGGIE DADDY : BUMPUS HOUNDS SCS 57, 12, 2 S/B HOTEL FROM 9:00 AM ( 1 HR NOTICE)

GRIP / ELECTRIC : RIGS + BATTERY PACS

TUTORING · 9:30 AM IN ROOM 512

CATERING: RUNNING SOUP + SANDWICH ON LOC A FOR 120 AT 1:00 PM
     LUNCH FOR 120 AT LOC B AT 5:00 PM

WEATHER · SUNNY INTERVALS HIGH 25°F, THURSDAY NIGHT CLEAR 15°F

ADVANCE SCHEDULE

| | | | | |
|---|---|---|---|---|
| EXT HOUSE | 12 pt | 3, 4 | | D |
| EXT FRONT PORCH | 46 pt | 1, 2, 3 | | D |
| EXT HOUSE | 51 COMP | 3, 4 | | D |
| EXT BACKYARD + ICELAND | 74 pt | 2, 3 | | D |

# Eating Pierogis

When my brother Jim first got involved with the film, he never dreamt
he would get to be in it, let alone in
what would be one of the most iconic
scenes in the movie. But that's exactly
what happened.

As I mentioned earlier, Rowley Inn is a bar that is
situated across the street from *A Christmas Story* House.
It was built around 1905 and was owned, at the time, by
our family friend, Teddy. It was always a shot-and-beer
place frequented mostly by steelworkers at all hours of
the day and night. Back then, two large mills, Republic
Steel and Jones and Laughlin Steel Corporations, were
down in the valley on the other side of the street. The Inn
was a very busy place, especially when Teddy prepared
his ethnic meals.

Around 7 one evening, Jim took a break from helping the movie crew. He was craving one of Teddy's most
popular dishes—pierogis. He entered the Rowley Inn,
prepared to have a feast. Several scenes were on schedule
for that night, including the Leg Lamp delivery scene. Julie, the local casting agent that Jim originally met when
he introduced her to the owner of the House, walked into
the bar. She needed four extras for different parts that
were being filmed at the house, and she needed them immediately. She was anxious. She didn't think it would be
easy to find four guys available so late in the evening.

Six years earlier, when *The Deer Hunter* was filmed
a few blocks away, it was summertime and there were
crowds of onlookers standing around watching the action. It was easy to find extras. Not so this time, on a
cold, wintry night.

Julie recognized Jim. She saw him and three other
guys at the bar and said, "How would you guys like to

be in the movie?" Jim jumped at the chance. He was also finished with his pierogis.

Julie signed up all four guys, right on the spot. Jim told her that he was already involved in the making of the film, so with Bob Clark's permission, Julie officially hired him up as a production assistant. That's the kind of luck Jim had, being in the right place at the right time. Additionally, I believe that eating pierogis brings good luck.

Jim was sent to the wardrobe department and outfitted with a cap, boots, gloves, and a jacket. Bob Clark said that Jim would be one of the delivery men. He was told to roll a dolly holding a crate along the porch and up to the front door. Jim was not told what was inside the crate.

Peter and Ian had no idea what was in the crate either. Only Bob Clark and a few of the crew members knew. That Leg Lamp was a closely kept secret. Bob Clark wanted to capture genuine looks of amazement from Ralphie and Randy. Watching their faces in the movie, it looks like he succeeded.

It was around 8 pm. Right at the start of the delivery scene, filming was delayed. No one had measured the front doorway before the crate was created. The crate was 6 feet tall and 4 feet wide, which was 4 inches wider than the front door of the House. Bob Clark called for the carpenters to cut two inches off each side of the crate. All they had nearby was a handsaw. Apparently the carpenters didn't hear Bob Clark, because they cut four inches off one side only.

As a result of the trimming, "THIS END UP" became "HIS END UP."

It didn't matter. Bob Clark was anxious to resume filming. The night was cold and it was late. Jim and another guy, also by the name of Jim, brought the large crate into the House.

To add to the confusion of the evening, the carpenters ran out of nails. To keep the crate together, they tied a large rope around the middle of it. In the movie, you can see Jim pushing the crate, with a rope around it, on the front porch. The script for that scene called for the crate to be nailed shut. In the movie, The Old Man tells Ralphie to get a crowbar and a hammer to assist in opening the crate.

A big rope tied around the crate was not in the script. Filming stopped again. Darren McGavin followed them out of the house and asked my brother Jim if he had a pocket knife to cut the rope. Jim did not. No one did. They couldn't get the rope off the crate.

It was around 10 pm. They were all tired. Bob Clark had enough. He said that they were done for the night and they could finish the scene later.

That "later" took place on a soundstage in Canada. It's movie magic—we see the crate with the rope around it on the porch, then the rope is mysteriously gone once it enters the house with two different delivery men. When the crate is laying on the floor, we can see it stamped as "HIS END UP." Bob Clark and his crew might have been frustrated by these little setbacks, but my brother Jim said he would have worked all night if they needed him.

I have a small figurine of the delivery man with the Fra-GEE-lay crate. It was created by Department 56, a manufacturer of *A Christmas Story* figurines and buildings. This little delivery man is dressed in the same outfit that Jim wore in the movie. It sits right by my keyboard to help me remember my promise to Jim to finish this book.

*A Christmas Story* figurine by Department 56

Jim & Fra-GEE-lay crate

*"A Christmas Story"*
January 27, 1983

*Jim Moralevitz*
(Freightman - extra)

# The White Cat

While watching a movie, especially a fast-paced one, we can forget that actual filming can be a long, sometimes tedious undertaking. After watching *A Christmas Story* being filmed, I learned this: while the scenes are being set up with all the cameras and lighting equipment in just the right position, the actors wait. They wait a lot.

The cast spends twice as many hours waiting for "action" as they spend actually acting.

When there are restless young actors with hours of time on their hands, there will be troubles on the set. One day during filming, they encountered more than trouble. There was an unexpected incident that really shook everyone to their core.

It all began when a very friendly little white cat started showing up around the set every day. Maybe it was star-struck. Peter Billingsley and Ian Petrella were captivated by that little guy. It was amazing how the cat ran to them when it saw them. Although that cat came to visit nearly every day, it stayed out of the way during filming.

(At least I think it stayed out of the way. Here's a challenge. Since I don't have the patience to try to find a white cat in the snow throughout the whole movie, I'll leave that undertaking to someone else. If you discover it, please let me know.)

Late one morning, as the scenes were being set up, Peter and Ian were playing with the cat when the cat decided to run away and explore the neighborhood. They innocently followed it down the street and out of the area of the House.

No one noticed them missing for quite some time. Everyone thought that they were somewhere else on the set. Then, Bob Clark asked to see Peter to talk about an upcoming scene. There were no cell phones back then, so the crew members went to find Peter. They searched all around the set. No one could find Peter. They looked in the wardrobe department. Not there. They went to look for Ian. He would know where to find Peter. But Ian was nowhere to be found. Ian was missing too!

Pure panic took over. Had they been kidnapped? Were they injured? If you have ever lost a child for even a moment, you can understand the fear and dread that instantly overcame everyone on set.

Bob Clark started bellowing orders to spread out and find them—NOW!

All the adults split up to search the streets, looking for the boys. Everyone was searching, shouting their names. Luckily, Jim knew the neighborhood. There's an alley behind Jim's house that's accessible from two streets and many backyards. When I was a child, the kids in my neighborhood called it "snake alley," because of its curvy shape. Jim quickly ran through the alley.

He saw Peter and Ian! They were further down the alley, trying to catch up with "their cat." Jim was so relieved. He wasn't upset with them, just grateful that nothing terrible had happened. He told them that everyone was frantically looking for them. The boys wanted to pick up the cat to take it back to the House, but it ran away. They had to leave it in the alley and walked back with Jim, safe and sound.

Jim saved the day!

Bob was so grateful to Jim that he gave him another job on the set: chaperone for those two boys. Jim was happy to help, as he was a very witty guy who always got along well with children. My children, Tim and Carol, adored him. When he came over to our house, all we heard was "Uncle Jim, Uncle Jim."

Peter and Ian liked Jim but they couldn't pronounce his last name correctly. They decided to call him "Mr. Jim." He loved that.

The boys were mostly well behaved, but keeping an eye

Peter Billingsley with the white cat

Ian Petrella (Randy) with the white cat

on them wasn't always an easy task. On three different occasions, Ian felt mischievous and hid from Jim. Jim remembers asking Peter, "Do you know where Ian is?" and Peter, with an innocent face, would say, "You're the one who's supposed to be watching us—don't you know, Mr. Jim?"

Jim once asked Ian why he was always hiding. Ian simply said, "I'm practicing for my part, Mr. Jim." Ian was talking about the famous scene where he hides under the kitchen sink. Hiding under the sink has become a ritual with many fans. Many of them get down on the floor and squeeze themselves into that tiny space when they visit the House.

Unfortunately for Bob Clark, Jim's role as chaperone for the boys ended when they retired to Stouffer's Hotel in downtown Cleveland each night. After work, Jim went to his home and his own bed. So as not to disrupt the downtown office traffic, the Christmas parade in the movie was filmed at 3 in the morning. The darkness also helped camouflage several high-rise buildings in that area. As a result, the children were kept up until late at night but were able to sleep late the next day. During this time, Higbee's Department Store did its business as usual until 6 p.m. The movie production crew worked through the nights.

In one iconic scene, Ralphie had to climb the steps of the Santa Mountain to see the jolly old elf. This mountain was over 30 feet tall. It took over three weeks to build stairs and construct a platform wide enough for Santa's chair and his helpers. The only way down from that mountain was down the slide. Fortunately, Higbee's had large rooms and high ceilings. It would be hard to put a 30-foot slide in many stores today! Higbee's kept the slide for several years after the movie was released, then sold it to Castle Noel, a Christmas-themed museum in Medina, Ohio.

The whole crew worked tirelessly to film that scene. To prevent people from using the slide during the day, a little white picket fence surrounded the mountain. As for the lights and cameras, they had to be taken down and put out of the way by morning. The only extras hired for the Santa scene were Higbee employees and their families. The store management could not risk having potential shoplifters meandering around all night long. They worked from 6 pm to 6 am for four consecutive nights. The main child actors were around the adults during the day, but they were mostly unsupervised during the night. On the nights that they weren't in the Santa or parade scenes, they became bored. What to do…what to do…

Well, they had a great time throwing water balloons from the upstairs windows onto pedestrians walking by. They also launched wet toilet paper rolls out onto passing cars. A few times, they called room service and ordered large amounts of food to be delivered to unsuspecting coworkers in the middle of the night.

Boys will be boys…

Making a movie seems glamorous to most of us, but it is, after all, a business and must be operated in an orderly, unglamorous fashion. Along with the many unique pictures in this book, you will find copies of the actual Call Sheets from Wednesday, January 26th and Thurs-

Peter Billingsley & R.D. Robb (Schwartz) with the white cat

Ralphie & Randy with film crew

Peter Billingsley hiding

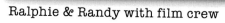

Running home from school

Ralphie

Randy & Ralphie

Ian Petrella (Randy) & Peter Billingsley (Ralphie) enjoying hot cocoa

day, January 27th, 1983. The Call Sheet from Thursday, January 27th has the adorable Bumpus Hounds on the schedule. Every day was different, and schedules were always changing to conform to the weather or to the actors.

There was a production meeting every morning. Jim joined makeup, wardrobe, and various crew members to discuss the schedule for that day. The Call Sheet was very meticulous as to who, what, when, and where. It contained a list of which actors were in scenes that day and what time they would be picked up from their hotel. It was essential that everyone know ahead of time just what needed to be done for that particular day. Transportation, locations, scene numbers, and cast are listed. There are details of the props, snow effects, vehicles, cameras, tutoring, catering, and the weather. It's incredible how organized they were. They had to be!

Jim took his job as Peter and Ian's chaperone very seriously. When Ian came back to Cleveland as a grown man, he remembered how nice Jim was to him during the filming of *A Christmas Story*.

In 2010, Ian came to Jim's 70th birthday party to join us in celebrating at (where else?) the Rowley Inn. Ian recalled one very cold day, after filming his iconic scene in which Randy says, "I can't put my arms down," he wanted hot cocoa. Jim made him a large mug of it. Jim then took a picture of Ian holding that mug, showing that Randy could, in fact, put his arms down. Ian autographed the picture at Jim's birthday party, signing: "It was great seeing you again, thanks for cocoa, oink oink, Ian Petrella (Randy)."

In that scene, Mrs. Parker is getting Randy bundled up to go outside. Randy is wearing so many layers that his arms stick straight out from his sides. This was achieved by duct taping blocks of upholstery foam under his arms, creating a comical spring when his mom pushed his arms down and they popped back up—very clever! The foam blocks were removed so that Ian could drink his cocoa. At his young age—he was a true professional actor.

# Peter Takes a Bath at Stella's

Growing up, my friends and I felt safe. We played outdoors both day and night. We never feared—our moms were near. These moms were shared by us all. They were constantly sticking their heads out of their doors to keep an eye on us. They made sure we ate, reprimanded our swearing, always knew where we were—and they definitely made sure we stayed out of trouble.

One of the moms who "adopted" me was Stella. She already had seven daughters of her own, but she once said to me, "What's one more?" Stella owned a home for many years on Buhrer Avenue, which is around the corner from *A Christmas Story* House. She was married to Stanley, and they raised ten children. Stella and my mom were very good friends. They had a lot in common. Both of them were of Polish descent, had many children, and were extremely strong-willed. Stella's youngest daughter, Chris, was my best friend in high school. When Chris married my brother Bob, we became one big happy family.

Stella excelled in the art of homemaking. She managed her home flawlessly. She was a talented cook, seamstress, nurse, and a diligent cleaner. She even scrubbed her basement floor on her hands and knees every week. Amazing!

Unbeknownst to Stella, she would play a pivotal role in the movie's Christmas Morning scene. Just not on camera.

Working outdoors in the cold for hours at a time was rough on all the workers, especially the children. Because the House was vacant, there was a generator attached to

a few small heaters inside. These heaters were not sufficient to warm a body.

In the Christmas Morning scene, Ralphie is so excited about receiving his cherished new rifle, he immediately runs outside in his pajamas and starts shooting at an old metal "Golden Age" advertising sign that's leaning against a trellis in his backyard. One of the BBs ricochets off the sign, hitting Ralphie in his cheek and knocking him down to the snow-covered ground. This snow was real and icy cold, as it came from one of the rented snow-making machines operating in the backyard. While the scene takes place in the morning, filming took place towards the end of the day, so large stadium lights were used for illumination.

Several takes of this scene were filmed, resulting in Peter falling into the snow several times. The snow began to saturate his pajamas. He was wearing long johns under his pajamas, but even those were damp and freezing cold. Soaked through, Peter began shivering. Peter's mom saw this and said to Director Bob Clark, "Stop filming. I'm going to take Peter back to the hotel now. He needs a warm bath to take the chill off."

It was getting late, and Bob was pressed for time. He wanted to finish that scene that day. If Peter went back to his room to take a bath at the hotel downtown, he would be gone for hours.

Bob had a great idea. He said, "Hey Jim, you live only a few houses away. How about letting Peter take a bath at your house? In the meantime, we'll get clean, dry clothes for him."

Jim said, "Sure. Let me go home and tidy my place up a bit." Jim ran home to straighten up his house, starting with the tub for Peter. When he walked into his bathroom and looked around, his heart sank. Jim realized that there was no way on earth he could let Peter, or Mrs. Billingsley for that matter, into his bathroom.

You see, Jim was a bachelor, and he really adored female anatomy. His bathroom walls were covered with *Playboy* playmate centerfold pictures. There were a lot of them. Everywhere.

Big pictures, too.

Jim was so anxious to help, he forgot all about them!

Jim started to panic. What to do? Who lives around here with a nice, clean bathroom? Then it came to him—Stella!

Jim called Stella. As it turned out, our mom was visiting her at the time. Jim said, "Hi Stella, I need to ask a favor of you. Can I bring Peter Billingsley over to your house to take a bath?"

Stella laughed. She knew that Jim was a big jokester. She said, "Hi Jim. Oh my, that's very funny. Your mom is here. Hold on—I'll get her for you."

Oh, this was not going the way he had hoped. Jim quickly said, "No, no, wait a minute—I'm serious." Then he explained what happened.

(Although he was never at a loss for words, Jim later told me that he had a real hard time explaining the *Playboy* pictures to Stella, who was a very strict Catholic.)

It took a while, but Stella was finally convinced that Jim wasn't joking. (He really was known for some over-the-top tales in his day.) She said, "Sure, bring that sweet boy over here before he catches a cold."

Jim, Peter, and Peter's mother rode in the limousine

Stella & Jim

Thank you card and letter (next page) courtesy of Chris Moralevitz

Stella & Me

past fifteen to twenty houses to reach Stella's. Peter was able to walk, but his mom asked Jim to carry him. Jim obligingly carried him up the front steps. His hands were full, so Jim banged on the door with his boot. My mom and Stella came running up to the door with wide eyes—Jim really was telling the truth!

Peter took a wonderful warm bath in Stella's impeccable bathroom. Meanwhile, his mom, our mom, Stella, and Jim sat at the kitchen table and had a nice chat over coffee and cake. Mrs. Billingsley talked easily with everyone. She already knew Jim, as they spoke occasionally while the movie was in production. While they were at Stella's house, all the crew members, a total of about 40 people, were waiting around for Peter to return. Jim said Bob Clark was calling him every 10 minutes on Stella's phone, asking, "Is he done yet? Is he done yet?"

After 45 minutes, Peter and Mrs. Billingsley returned to *A Christmas Story House*, both of them very warm and happy. Filming commenced, and Ralphie was able to finish the Christmas Morning scene. Shortly after this, Stella received a large bouquet of beautiful flowers in a very pretty vase. Attached was a thank-you card from Peter and his mom. The note said, "Thank you for your hospitality and your bathtub." She also received a reproduced handwritten two-page fan letter from Peter in which he said that his favorite food was pizza and French fries. He mentions his goals—that he will act until he's eighteen, then become a lifeguard, a ski patrol at age 21, a football player, a doctor, then finally own a pizza store. He also wrote that he had a dog named Brandy and a turtle named Teddy. It's a very sweet letter and on display in *A Christmas Story* Museum.

Stella loved receiving the flowers, but she really was just happy she was able to help. For years, she proudly displayed the vase, note, and fan letter in her home for all to see.

Several years later, when Jim found out that he was about to become a grandfather, the *Playboy* pictures finally came down from their places of prominence.

# Peter Billingsley

1982

Dear Friend,

Thank you for your letter. It is hard for me to write each of my fans seperate letters while I'm going to school and working. Every letter is very special to me. In this letter I will try to answer some questions I'm asked a lot.

When I'm not working I go to school and do the things we all are expected to do, like cleaning my room and doing the dishes. I'm in the Fifth grade. When I'm working at a studio or on location I have school for about 3 hrs. a day with a teacher. I attend public school when I'm not working. I like both types of school. When I'm working there is more attention, and at regular school there are more kids to play with. My favorite color is purple. My favorite foods are pizza and french fries. I'm on a baseball team in the spring and a football team in the fall. I also love riding my minibike off the road, going rollerskating, swimming, playing outside, and playing video games. My favorite T.V. shows are "Dukes of Hazard" and of course, "Real People".

I started acting when I was 3 years old and would like to continue until I'm about 18. Then I want to be a life guard and a ski patrol. Then when I'm about 21 I want to be a football player and then be a doctor and finally I want to own a pizza store. I have two brothers and two sisters and they are also actors.

We have a dog named Brandy and a turtle named Teddy. I am eleven years old and my birthday is April 16, 1971. I will try to keep in touch with you as much as I can. Thankyou for writing and most of all, being my friend.

I'm happy to send a picture and letter to any of your friends if they write to me at the address below.

With all my best Wishes,
Peter

NBC TV
3000 WEST ALAMEDA AVE.
BURBANK, CA   91523

# Hollywood, Here We Come!

The acting bug entered my home the day my daughter, Carol, was called upon by Bob Clark to be the only girl in the opening scene.

Most movie scenes are not filmed in the exact chronological order of the manuscript. Availability of the actors, the weather, and location dictate which scenes will be filmed on any particular day.

At the last minute, Bob Clark wanted to include a girl in the opening scene that featured Ralphie and his friends. In this scene, the kids are running past a dilapidated fence on their way home from school. There were lots of girls in other movie scenes, but for some reason they didn't have a female child actress available for that day. Bob Clark knew that Jim had family in the Cleveland area, so he asked Jim if he knew of a girl who was Peter's age.

Jim said, "Yes, my niece, Carol—she's ten years old." Jim called me that day.

When I picked up the phone, Jim was laughing excitedly. He said, "Sis, can you bring Carol over here on Thursday? Bob Clark would like to shoot a scene that includes a girl around the age of ten." We were so excited! Carol was going to be in a Hollywood movie! Carol was on cloud nine. I was so happy for her. I was also hoping I would meet Darren McGavin and Melinda Dillon. My mom was staying with us at the time and—oh boy—she instantly had Hollywood on her mind. I think she was already planning on moving into our Beverly Hills mansion with us.

Because the filming was on a school day, Carol needed to take time off school. I stopped by her school to see Mrs. Taft, her teacher. I excitedly told her about Carol's great opportunity to be in a movie. We both agreed that

Carol & Peter

it would be a wonderful life lesson for her. Since Carol was such a good student, her teacher gave her consent and said, "I'm so thrilled for you!"

Although we were all very excited at the time, we really thought it would be just another children's Christmas movie. No one could possibly fathom just how enormously popular it would turn out to be. Carol told all her little friends that this was going to be her very first "job." We brought our son, Tim, with us. We were hoping that they might need an adorable 4-year-old as an extra. Unfortunately, no small children were in this scene. Nevertheless, Tim was a well-behaved little trooper throughout that long day.

We were told to report to the set early that Thursday morning. We all met Julie, the casting director. We signed permission forms for Carol to work eight hours. Carol officially had a job in the movie! The only people I recognized were my friend Lorna and her son Michael, who also was around ten years old. Lorna was, and still is, married to Teddy, owner of the Rowley Inn at that

My mom & Carol

Carol on the set

time. She was later cast in a scene with The Old Man and Swede. She is the pretty lady standing by Swede, with her son Michael. They were across the street from the House, admiring the Leg Lamp in the front window.

There was a friendly atmosphere in the makeshift green room. I remember making small talk with the other mothers and guardians while we had coffee and doughnuts. The paperwork and wardrobe transactions for everyone who was working that day took up most of the morning and afternoon. Around midday, we drove to a hilly sidewalk in the Tremont area of Cleveland, not far from the House itself. The lighting technicians and cameramen were all set. The actual script title for that scene was: "Kids run past dilapidated fence." It was an exterior dusk scene.

Here's the scene: Carol, Ralphie, Flick, and Randy run alongside a large wooden dilapidated fence in the alley, with the steel mills in the background. It was the opening scene to the movie.

My mom, Bob, Tim, and I stood quietly on the side-lines and watched patiently. There were many takes for that scene. It took all evening. There was a whole lot of "hurry up and wait." Then it was over. That was a day none of us will ever forget. This was our daughter Carol's

Carol's autographed fan photo

first job! She was paid for eight hours of work.

After coming with us to the set to watch Carol "act," Mom came down with a case of "Movie Madness." She was so delighted! Mom was always a talker, but that day she just sat quietly and took it all in. I think she had visions of Carol being the next Shirley Temple. Although they didn't film my mom, she talked about her "movie experience" for years.

I took a picture of my mom with Carol as they were standing by one of the antique automobiles. Carol certainly looked like a girl from the 1930s in her costume. Wardrobe provided her with a knee-length gray woolen coat, a maroon scarf, and a red knitted beanie. She also had on black leggings, white socks, and black rubber boots. As it turned out, my mom was already wearing an old-fashioned coat with a fur collar that looked like it was made in the 30s. It was her coat for special occasions. She fit right in.

When you visit the *Christmas Story* Museum, you can see that picture of my mom and Carol alongside that 1937 Oldsmobile Touring Sedan, one of the many vintage cars used in the movie. I remember seeing the proud owners of these cars standing around and watching the actors, waiting for the car scenes. They were filmed driving their own classic cars.

When *A Christmas Story* opened in the theaters on Friday, November 18, 1983, we were tremendously excited! We could not wait to see Carol on the big screen. We arrived in time for the second showing. As we were walking up the aisle of our neighborhood theater, who did we see? Carol's teacher—Mrs. Taft! She had just seen the movie and said sadly, "I kept looking for Carol, but I never saw her."

I replied, "It wasn't a big part, you were probably looking too hard," and laughed. Well, we never saw Carol appear in the movie either. Unfortunately, her part in the scene ended up on the editing room floor. We were so sad. We couldn't believe it. Carol was disappointed, but she put on a brave face. I explained to her that it certainly wasn't her acting, and that sometimes these things just happen. She understood and was satisfied with the fact that she got the chance of a lifetime to almost be in a

Ralphie, Flick, & Schwartz

Hollywood movie.

All movies are edited for mistakes or to make the movie fit a certain time slot. As the story goes, MGM wanted to keep this movie around 90 minutes long so it could be shown every two hours in the theater. It is the editors' choice what stays in the film. I have looked, and been told, that the edited film scenes with Carol in them were destroyed. I found the next best thing: a copy of the original script for the opening of the movie.

Jean Shepherd wanted the opening scene to feature the massive steel mills' smokestacks in the far distance. His original manuscript depicted the opening scene showing the children running past a slag pile at the steel mills, then past a dilapidated fence. This was the scene Carol was in, #2 Ext. Junkyard—Dusk. The actual movie instead shows the steel mills in the background of the opening scene, but they are behind the house, not the children.

In the 25th Anniversary of *A Christmas Story* DVD documentary, casting director Julie Matthews mentioned that she had a part as a caroler in the downtown parade scene of the movie. Unfortunately, she ended up on the editing room floor also—and she was the casting director!

On the bright side, we do have many pictures and wonderful memories of that day. Peter autographed his picture and gave it to Carol. To top it off, we were able to spend the day with Director Bob Clark, who was truly a down-to-earth, wonderful guy.

We also have bragging rights. To this day, if the subject of the movie or the House comes up in conversation, I will mention the part that Carol played and everyone gets really excited and asks me to tell them the whole story.
The filming of this movie in Cleveland in early 1983 just lifted the winter doldrums right off everyone. The whole city was energized!
But all good things do come to an end. It truly was a gloomy and depressing day when the crews packed up the trucks, rolled right off our street, and out of Cleveland.
I could feel the sadness in the air.
It was a wild ride, and it was over.

# The House

While searching through several boxes looking for all my *A Christmas Story* photographs for this book, I came across an adorable photo of me at age two. Behind me is my brother Bob and in the background is the house that would become world-famous. I realized that the house has been a part of my life, all of my life, and took it as a sign that this book is meant to be. I do not remember the moment that photo was taken, but I do remember being around five years old when I first visited the house that would someday become the *Christmas Story* House.

This house was built in 1895 as a two-family structure. One of my childhood playmates, Mary, lived on the first floor. I mostly remember her long, dark hair. I loved going over to her house to play—she had a lot more toys than I did! She was an only child and had her own bedroom. Coming from my tiny home with seven brothers and sisters, I was in awe. We spent many winter nights playing with our dolls.

Several years after Mary moved away, another friendly family moved into the House. I remember a girl named Renee, who was about a year younger than I. She also lived on the first floor. I fondly recall one Halloween when Renee's mom bought several small pumpkins and asked me if I ever had made a jack-o'-lantern. When I said "no," she handed me my very own little pumpkin and taught me how to carve. She even let me take my little masterpiece home. She was a very nice lady. I think of that kind-hearted woman and my first experience carving up my little pumpkin without cutting off my fingers every time I visit *A Christmas Story House* and enter that kitchen. It looks quite different now. All my memories of being in that house are joyful ones. I don't recall if we ever hid under the sink. I believe it was a different sink then.

When I was a teenager, I would visit my friend Thelma, who lived on the second-story floor of the House. There was a party going on every weekend. Our Saturday night began with a walk to a neighborhood restaurant. There weren't very many at that time so our choices were limited. Whoever we saw on our way home would be invited to our party at Thelma's that night.

Most of the time, we listened to our records or turned on the radio and just danced. We would drink our beers and dance for hours. Thelma was older so she would drink wine once in a while. To avoid incriminating myself or others, let me just say that I almost never got into trouble.

When I first took a tour of the House, it was very strange to see Ralphie's bedroom being upstairs at the front of the house. That's where Thelma's living room was. Back then, I would open the screen in the front window, lean out, and call out to any friends I saw passing by or coming out of Rowley Inn. I'd tell them to come on up and dance! I remember going up the stairway to her house through the back door. There was no front door to the second floor. Because it was a two-family home at the time of production, all the indoor scenes in the movie were filmed on a soundstage in Canada. When Brian purchased the House, he renovated the whole structure. He joined the two floors by installing a staircase in the middle of the house to duplicate the house in the movie.

The last person who owned the House when it was still just a regular house was a very sweet and loving guy named Joe. Joe was a dear friend of my brothers, my husband, and me. He worked for the Cleveland Water Department. Joe was around seven to eight years older than me. We first met through mutual friends when he moved to a small house a few blocks away. As a teenager, I had a huge crush on Joe. He was so doggone nice and, I might add, handsome. Years later, I was surprised to learn from my brother Jim that Joe and his brothers bought that house, which was still just a regular two-family home. The purchase price was $46,000 in the year 2000. Joe only lived there a few years before he passed away. Not long after Joe's death, his brothers Alan and Kenneth, rented out the House. They noticed that people would drive by the House, stop, and talk about the movie that was made there so many years ago.

The movie became more popular each year due to the marathons on television every Christmas. In December of 2004, Joe's brothers decided to sell the house. With the help of a friend who was a part-time Realtor, Alan posted the house on eBay. In the eBay listing, they emphasized that it was once the home of Ralphie Parker! The asking price for the house was $99,900. That was an outrageous price, considering the neighborhood. Brian called the brothers and took a gamble, spending $150,000 cash on the 1895 home, sight unseen!

As the story goes, Brian Jones loved *A Christmas Story*, and he especially loved the Leg Lamp. Brian's parents built a replica of the Leg Lamp for him in order to cheer him up after he was unable to become a Navy pilot, due to his poor eyesight. In 2003, he launched a very lucrative company called the "Red Rider Leg Lamps" in San Diego. Orders were placed through an online website selling "Red Rider Leg Lamps" exclusively. Evidently there are a whole lotta Leg Lamp lovers in this world, because from just the sale of the lamps alone, Brian made enough money to buy the House.

Brian Jones' wife, Beverly, a surface warfare officer, was aboard a naval amphibious assault ship headed for the Middle East. The captain of the ship saw the house listed on eBay, remembered Brian's involvement with the Leg Lamp, and showed the listing to Beverly. She then told Brian, as she knew he'd be interested. After all, he was making good money selling the Leg Lamps. Although he didn't even know where Cleveland, Ohio was, Brian was definitely interested.

Alan and Kenneth must have thought it was a practical joke. It was no joke, but I'm sure that they laughed all the way to the bank! Brian flew to Cleveland and saw the House in person for the first time on December 28, 2004. Someone offered the brothers $200,000 a few months after they agreed to sell it to Brian. We'll never know what that person would have done with the House, but I'm grateful that Alan and Kenneth stuck to their agreement with Brian.

Just to give you an idea of the real estate market in that neighborhood, my mom and dad tried to sell our family home back in 1973, and the most they could get for it was $7,000. At the time Brian bought the House, the surrounding homes, both single and two-family, could not sell for anything over $50,000. The neighborhood was on a decline that continued into the 2000s. That did not deter Brian. He became the proud owner of the *Christmas Story House* on January 31, 2005. His goal was to replicate the House exactly as it had looked in the movie.

A whole lot of work, time, and elbow grease transformed the inside. The same could be said for restoring the outside. That included tearing down the gray vinyl, installing windows to match the ones in the movie, and repairing the original shed. One of the first projects was cutting a hole through the second floor in the middle of the house for the staircase. Since Brian's dream was to make it look exactly as it did in the movie, he had to transform this duplex into a one-family home.

The renovations are incredible. It took Brian and Beverly Jones two years to transform the old two-family home into the Parker home. Every visitor can now experience what it feels like to be in "Ralphie's house." I believe Bob Clark would have loved it. It would have made filming the movie a lot easier if those renovations were done back in 1983.

At the time of purchase, my brother Jim still lived in our childhood home a few doors down. He would stop by the House to watch the renovations. When Brian Jones arrived to look at his newly purchased home, Jim walked right up and welcomed him to the neighborhood. Jim did that to every new neighbor—after all, he was the Mayor of West 11th Street. They became fast friends due to a big common interest: anything and everything connected to *A Christmas Story*. They would talk for hours on end about the movie. Brian wanted to learn everything he could about how it was back then and Jim was like a human encyclopedia of what went on behind the cameras. When Jim told his many stories, he would always, and I mean always, smile. He would get so detailed about the events he witnessed that he made everyone feel like they were there with him. It was like he painted with his words.

When I first spoke to Brian, he told me that Jim was a "valuable link between then and now" and how grateful he was for Jim's help. He once told me that Jim's passion for the project and memories of that time were an incredible asset to Brian.

It certainly didn't look like Ralphie's house when Brian Jones bought it. While he was living there, Joe had a lot of improvements made. The house had new windows and a new roof. The original wood siding was covered with gray vinyl. The shed that was filmed in the dream scene was still standing, but it was in a state of disrepair. Brian Jones painstakingly renovated the house and property by investing an additional $240,000. He also purchased the house that my cousin John once lived in, located across the street from the House, for $129,000 and turned it into *A Christmas Story* Museum. This Museum also served as a gift shop when it was first opened to the public.

Brian Jones' dream had become a reality.

*A Christmas Story* House kitchen

Mom's antique orange juicer (top shelf on right)

# After *A Christmas Story*

*A Christmas Story* had a rough start at the theaters. According to Bob Clark, MGM Studios didn't give it a chance. It was only played in only 100 theaters around the country during the two weeks surrounding Christmas. It didn't help that the movie critics were unkind.

In his review of the movie, the critic Roger Ebert said, "My guess is either nobody will see it, or millions of people will see it." Now, I know this movie was never intended to win an Oscar, but I have seen some Christmas movies that were far worse and had nothing to do with good will. The fact that this once-ridiculed movie is now so deeply loved by people all over the world has a redeeming, Christmassy quality to it, wouldn't you say?

Warner Brothers bought the rights to *A Christmas Story* in 1986 from MGM. Due to the increasing popularity of the film, TNT began airing a 24-hour marathon dubbed "24 Hours of *A Christmas Story*" in 1997. The film was shown twelve consecutive times beginning at 7 pm on Christmas Eve and ending Christmas Day. Bob Clark stated that in 2002, an estimated 38.4 million people tuned into the marathon at one point or another, nearly one-sixth of the country. The number of people who have tuned in is now over 50 million!

In many homes, *A Christmas Story* is the soundtrack of Christmas Eve and Christmas Day. Many children born since 1997 have never known a Christmas without it.

As for my old neighborhood changing after *A Christmas Story*, it is really due to the renovation of *A Christmas Story* House, along with its additional museum and gift shop. Opening Day was a day I will always remember. Seeing hundreds of people converge on my once very quiet street truly felt dreamlike to me.

Take, for instance, what was happening in the house next to the *Christmas Story House* on its opening day. A clever 10-year-old boy sold Ovaltine out of an 18-quart roaster he set up on his front lawn. He wore a Scut Farkus coonskin hat and Ralphie glasses. He also had a Red Ryder BB gun nearby. He was ready! This young man's mom was sitting nearby with eight-week-old puppies that she jokingly advertised as Bumpus hounds. They weren't real hound dogs, but they were adorable. Looking back, I realize that there was a window of opportunity that no one thought of—Bumpus hound dogs' descendants could have been sold for top dollar that day. After all, a line from the movie stated that "the Bumpuses had over 785 smelly hounds."

Teddy sold the Rowley Inn in 2014. The most recent owner is Jon, who purchased it in 2016. It has been renovated into a modern restaurant and bar. The front wall of the building was revamped by putting in a large picture window. There is, of course, a large Leg Lamp shining brightly in that window, which also offers a great view of *A Christmas Story* House and Museum. It is a great place to watch the fans from the comfort of a cozy bar.

Jon offers an array of dinners and specialty drinks relating to the movie. A very popular dinner special is Randy's Meatloaf Dinner, which is meatloaf served over roasted garlic mashed potatoes, topped with peppered gravy and onion straws with a side of grilled broccoli. One of the bourbon drinks is a Triple Dog Dare Ya, which consists of Crown Apple, Crown Vanilla, Pinnacle Whipped Cream Vodka, Horchata Liqueur, and Cinnamon Bitters, topped with Maine Root Beer. There are several other dinners to choose from, including the time-honored pierogis, a big favorite. I'm grateful that he kept the original hand-made wooden bar, which will probably outlast all of us. Now, almost 40 years later, there are only a handful of neighbors who were around when the movie was filmed back in 1983.

Visiting *A Christmas Story* House and Museum is an experience you'll always remember. It's so realistic, you can almost believe that Darren McGavin will be sitting in the kitchen! A Christmas tree is standing in the corner of the living room year-round. Ralphie's beloved rifle is in the opposite corner. The world-famous Leg Lamp stands in all its splendor in front of the large picture window in the living room. Brian didn't miss a thing.

When Brian was getting the House ready for public viewing, he needed articles from the 1940-1950s. Jim knew that I collected antiques and asked me if I had anything to donate. I was happy to contribute my dad's brown desk lamp that he had for over fifty years. It was on a desk in the living room of the House when it first opened. I also donated my mom's antique orange juicer, which still sits on a shelf in the kitchen, over the stove. And, I donated a beautiful doily that my Aunt Mary crocheted. It's draped across the back of one of the couches in the living room of the House.

The second floor was beautifully renovated. It includes Ralphie and Randy's bedroom. It looks exactly like the one in the movie. In addition to the bedrooms, there is also a sewing room with an ironing board in it. That room is not in the movie, but it does add an old-fashioned feel to the House. It is the only room in the House that is not interactive.

In the bathroom, the Little Orphan Annie decoder is there by the toilet, for anyone who wants to try to decode the message themselves. There is a tablet with the words "Be sure to drink your Ovaltine" written on it. There is a bar of vintage red Lifebuoy soap just like the one used to wash out Ralphie's mouth, although the actual "soap" that Mrs. Parker made Ralphie put in his mouth was a bar of wax.

The Red Ryder BB gun was named after a comic

Mom's antique orange juicer
(top shelf on right)

Aunt Mary's crocheted doily
(sofa on left)

strip cowboy and was first produced in 1938. There were six original Red Ryder rifles used by Ralphie in the movie. Peter Billingsley, a leftie, owns the actual left-handed rifle that he used in the movie. In November, 2016, Brian Jones obtained another of the originals, displayed in a glass case. Brian called it a "holy grail" for the Museum. A third rifle is rumored to be hidden in Hollywood. There are still three of them unaccounted for. Here's how to tell that it's an original: The Daisy manufacturing company has produced Red Ryder 200-shot carbine action rifles since 1940. Jean Shepherd's version existed only in his mind. Daisy Outdoor Products produced the Red Ryder BB gun, but it didn't have a sundial and compass attached. Those features were made up by Jean Shepherd. Its complete name in the movie is "An Official Daisy Red Ryder 200-shot Carbine Action Range Model Air Rifle."

That is only one of the many genuine movie props on display in the museum, including the original pink bunny suit and rhinestone cowboy outfit. Whenever I visit the *Christmas Story* House and Museum, I cannot believe how many people I see with their cameras constantly clicking! To add to the ambiance, you'll hear an antique floor model radio playing Ralphie's favorite radio shows. There are also knowledgeable, friendly tour guides. You can touch anything in the House, but everything in the Museum is under glass. They are happy to take a picture of you in bunny ears, standing on the landing of the steps. There is the infamous telephone on the hallway wall—someone is always using it as a prop for their pictures. Pick up the phone receiver and you can hear a recording of the phone call between Ralphie's mother and Mrs. Schwartz that took place in the movie. This conversation results from Peter telling his mom that Schwartz taught him "the queen mother of dirty words."

Fans love the original shed in the back and can see where Ralphie nearly shot his eye out with his beloved Red Ryder BB gun.

Whenever I visit the gift shop, I am overwhelmed at

the different kinds of merchandise. There's always something new. All around the shop are Leg Lamp images stamped on glasses, ties, jewelry, clothing, plates, games, costumes, and many other items too numerous to mention. There are sections displaying items from other classic movies, like *Elf, The Nightmare Before Christmas* and *National Lampoon's Christmas Vacation.*

Most of the display tables are in the shape of wooden crates that are labeled "FRAGILE." My first time there, I did not expect that. Seeing so many of these crates made me miss Jim more, as I have and always will associate that crate with Jim.

The movie is played on big-screen televisions located in the House, Museum, and Store. It is played over and over again on each and every day that these buildings are open to the public, which is almost every day. I wonder how the workers feel about that. I also wonder if they have the lines memorized by now. The tour guides are everywhere, happily assisting the fans in making it a visit to remember.

A few years ago, I met Steven Intermill, who was the very efficient curator of *A Christmas Story* Museum for several years. He went on to own and operate the Buckland Museum of Witchcraft and Magick. We've spoken at length on several occasions about the movie and about Jim. While working at *A Christmas Story* Museum, Steven did a marvelous job of obtaining long-lost newspaper and magazine articles pertaining to the movie.

In the Museum you will find a lot of the movie's clothing, including Randy's "I can't put my arms down" snowsuit. There's also the mailbox where Ralphie discovered his long-awaited Ovaltine letter.

According to the documentary *Road Trip For Ralphie* by Tyler and Jordie Schwartz, several of the original vintage clothing the kids wore in the movie was discovered in Toronto, Canada. They found many of the outfits in a costume shop called Thunder Thighs, run by a woman named Lynda, who personally knitted many of the hats and scarves that we see in the movie, including Randy's very long scarf. When Brian Jones learned of this, he flew to Toronto and bought the entire collection for *A Christmas Story* Museum. What a stroke of good luck! Several antique toys from the Higbee's windows are on display in showcases. Some of the wind-ups still work! Also on display throughout the Museum are numerous pictures that were shot during the movie. The complete set of Jim's pictures, combined with mine, are enclosed in this eye-opening book that you are holding in your hands this very minute!

Brian Jones and Steven Intermill arranged the display of a wooden panel of an oversized "FRAGILE" crate on the wall in the front room where Jim captivated audiences with his stories for many years. Rare photos taken by Jim, my husband Bob, and me are showcased on this large panel. To honor Jim's dedication to *A Christmas Story* movie and Museum, there is a wooden plaque above the panel—a carving of Jim and the Leg Lamp. An inscription at the bottom reads: "To Susie-Q, Bob and Timmy Too. THIS END UP! WOW! Who'd a thunk it? Love, Jim." Bob and I cried when we saw that we were included in this commemoration. Unfortunately, Steven was not in the Museum the first time we saw it, so I called Brian and Steven to thank them for being so kind and considerate. We are beyond grateful to them.

Tickets to view the House are sold in the Museum. I mentioned earlier that I paid $5.00 in 2006 to tour the *Christmas Story* House. Ticket prices have gone up, due to inflation and the fact that the museum is always expanding with additional one-of-a-kind memorabilia from the movie donated from fans and finds on eBay.

Behind the *Christmas Story* Museum is a 1937 Oldsmobile Touring Sedan, safely tucked inside a garage. It was in the Christmas parade scene in the film and looks similar to the Parker family car. Fans love to take selfies in front of an antique fire truck, also kept in the garage. It's not the one in the movie, but it does set the period for the movie and is really cool.

When leaving the House, be sure to look up at the light pole across the street. There is a simple but significant tribute to Jean Shepherd, the creator of *A Christmas Story*. Attached to the West 11th Street sign is another street sign: "Cleveland Street." Mr. Shepherd's childhood home was located on Cleveland Street in Hammond, Indiana. How ironic; from Cleveland Street to Cleveland, Ohio.

Jim's wooden plaque & photo display cases in the museum

# It's Always Something

*A Christmas Story* has left a mark beyond the House and Museum. The C&Y Chinese Restaurant on St. Clair Avenue wasn't in the movie, but they were caught up in the spirit of it. During 2006, they actually served the roasted Peking duck with the head still intact, then chopped it off tableside with a giant meat cleaver! I never had the nerve to experience it. *A Christmas Story* was constantly shown on a big screen television in this restaurant, and a ticket stub from the House got you a 20% discount off your meal. Unfortunately, this restaurant closed years ago.

In 2008, the actual fire truck that was used in the Christmas parade in the movie, a 1938 Ward LaFrance pump truck, came to Cleveland and toured the neighborhood. Excited fans stood in the back of the truck. There is a different fire truck that arrived to come to Flick's aid when his tongue was stuck to the flagpole. That truck is currently stored at Chippawa Volunteer Firefighters Association station in Niagara Falls, Canada. It is available for viewing every Sunday.

The historic Higbee building was sold and restored to its original beauty, but instead of becoming a department store once again, it became the Horseshoe Casino. In 2016 the Horseshoe was bought by Mr. Danny Gilbert and the name was changed to Jack. Every Christmas season from 2012 through the present, the casino's owners graciously re-create several storefront windows with *A Christmas Story* toys similar to what was seen in the movie.

The inside of this magnificent building was once illuminated with 18 Leg Lamps and 21 original trees from Higbee's Department Store. There were also garland-strung archways covering the first floor, just like it was at Higbee's when I was young. They have scaled back the decorations in the last few years.

The first convention for *A Christmas Story* was held in the downtown Renaissance Cleveland Hotel, where the cast stayed in 1983, although it was called Stouffer's Inn on the Square then. This convention took place on November 23rd and 24th, 2007. That coincided with the Thanksgiving weekend festivities held each year, marking the beginning of the Christmas season by lighting up the trees and buildings downtown.

My brother Jim was there to join in the festivities and recollected his behind-the-scenes stories again and again. He always made the stories feel brand new. Many of the actors stayed at that hotel and met the fans for autographs on the first floor. A fleet of street trolleys, called Lolly the Trolley, provided round-trip transportation between the Renaissance Hotel and *A Christmas Story* House and Museum during the convention weekend.

The actress who portrayed the tough little elf in the movie, Patty Johnson, sold red and green felt elf hats she had sewn herself. According to her Fox 8 news interview, the casting director was looking for an actor with a really bad attitude to play the "hurry up kid" elf. Patty Johnson had a great audition, the casting director loved her and hired her the next day.

An attraction at that 2007 convention was a "Chinese turkey dinner" and a BB-gun shooting range. The original classroom door and slate blackboard from Victoria School were also on display at this convention. Victoria school was once located in St. Catharines, Ontario, Canada and was featured as the Warren G. Harding Elementary School in the movie. It's incredible how this movie has affected so many people, that they gladly salvage the props and items. Unfortunately, the famous metal flagpole was demolished for a housing project.

In 2013, at *A Christmas Story* 30th anniversary convention, a musical and a play based on the movie were shown. There was also *A Christmas Story* memorabilia auction. A big attraction for the children that year was a "Mrs. Parker's Little Piggy Luncheon." This luncheon featured the traditional meatloaf and mashed potato dinner. Some of the cast members were included. I hope a lot of napkins were on hand. Where else can you enjoy a dinner like that but in Cleveland!

There are many internet reviews of the *Christmas Story* House in which people comment about how dangerous the neighborhood looked. In reality, it is more poor than dangerous. Many neighbors are hard-working people who are just trying to make ends meet. The ever-creative Brian Jones raises money through his nonprofit foundation to help the neighbors remodel their homes. He set up *A Christmas Story* House Neighborhood Restoration Project.

It works with Tremont West Development Corporation to provide the necessary funds for repairs. It is very attainable to those in need. The homeowners simply fill out a form describing what they need financial help with. There are remarkable before-and-after photos on the nonprofit's website. Many of the neighbors have been deeply moved by the generosity of the foundation. Some could not otherwise afford their much-needed home restorations. For many years since the conventions were cancelled, the nonprofit's largest fundraiser is *A Christmas Story* 5K and 10K Run. This festive and fun one-of-a-kind run starts in downtown Cleveland in front of the Higbee's building and ends at *A Christmas Story* House.

The mailbox in front of *A Christmas Story* House is the 5K finish and the turning point for the 10K runners. Thousands of people participate, many of them running in Leg Lamp costumes—complete with fishnet stockings. There are also many pink bunny outfits and Black Bart costumes. With the help of benefactors and volunteers, over $300,000 has been raised since 2013. Runners mill about after the race, drinking beer in The Old Man's tent or drinking Ovaltine. Six hundred gallons of Ovaltine were given out at the finish line in 2017. While recuperating from the run and relaxing around *A Christmas Story* House, Museum and Gift Shop, the runners can see where their money is going by viewing the renovations of the homes in that area.

My husband Bob and I participated in the 2019 Christmas Story 5K Run, held on December 7, 2019. We are not runners, but—what the heck—it's a worthwhile fundraiser. For the first time in our lives, we wore matching outfits. We both wore pajama bottoms featuring Ralphie and a bar of soap. (The theme that year was "Oh Fuuuudge.") We also wore the long-sleeved red shirts that were provided for all participants, with the *Christmas Story* logo on the front and the names of racing sponsors on the back.

We did not see Brian that day, but we did see hundreds of pink bunnies and Leg Lamps congregate in Cleveland public square. Babies and dogs were dressed up as Black Barts and Christmas trees. Many people were wearing Ralphie's beanie hats and Scut Farkus' raccoon-skin hats. There were several kids dressed up like Randy, unable to put their arms down. It was a sight and experience like no other. A few days before, I texted Brian and asked him if there was a prize for last place. He said no, nor for the middle place, which is where he usually ends up. Well, Bob and I were actually in last place. The security car was right behind us. We reached the 1-mile marker and called it a day. Will I do it again? Most definitely. I have a whole year to get in shape. Maybe next year I will make it 2 miles.

Many Cleveland-area businesses are involved with helping with the run. They help to make it a fun and very enjoyable way to raise money. Cleveland's own Jack Frost Donuts developed a line of *A Christmas Story*-themed donuts. These donuts are sold for a limited time, usually from early November until December 26th. One of their newest creations is a donut in the shape of the "FRAGILE" crate. I guess I'll have to make a special trip to Jack Frost Donuts just to see what that crate tastes like.

Jim would have been tickled about that donut. They also have a Leg Lamp, Red Ryder rifle, and pink bunny donuts. They donate 5% of their profits to the Christmas Story Foundation. Sweet!

That Leg Lamp crate is so popular, it has gone viral. There is a Lego piece shaped like the crate with "FRAG-ILE" on it!

For several years, the Cleveland Play House has presented *A Christmas Story* play, adapted from the movie. It is held at the Allen Theatre. We relive the narrator's walk down memory lane and Ralphie Parker's wistful dreaming of the Red Ryder air rifle. It's great to see the movie come to life every year.

To experience the movie on the big screen, just like I did in 1983, the Capitol Theater on Cleveland's west side runs the film on weekends in December. Admission is only $1.00. That's about what I paid in 1983. They also request a donation of a non-perishable food item for the Greater Cleveland Food Bank. It is incredible how this movie continues to give to the needy, decades after it was made. Because of the good people of Northeast Ohio, I believe it will continue to give for decades to come.

One of the original reasons I wanted to write this book was to show the ripple effect of how the decisions and actions of a few can affect the lives of many. First, there was the location scout's decision to pick that house. Next, there was Bob Clark's decision to film the movie there. Years later, it was Brian's decision to open the house to the public. The culmination of those choices truly put Cleveland on the map for tourists' destinations, especially at Christmas.

I have seen, firsthand, the heavy traffic from tourists all year round, and from the day after Thanksgiving to early January, an average of 45,000 people from all over the world converge on our little neighborhood. They faithfully wait in long lines, as the tour is 30 minutes long, or longer. Everyone has more than enough time to get their *Christmas Story* "fix." Many families have made visiting *A Christmas Story* House a yearly tradition.

A two-disc DVD set commemorating *A Christmas Story* is called: "25th Anniversary of *A Christmas Story*/25th Anniversary Convention in Cleveland." This set was created and produced by Mr. Tyler Schwartz.

On the first disc, the panel of speakers consisted of my brother Jim, Dwayne (Black Bart), Julie Matthews (casting agent) and Paul Zaza, who composed the music soundtrack for the movie. In this documentary, Jim talks about some of the contributions he made while the movie was being filmed. He was being modest.

In the documentary, it was so nice to see Jim blush when he received compliments after his speech. Mr. Schwartz said to Jim, "You had a small role, but you're one of the biggest personalities to come out of this movie."

When Mr. Schwartz asked the audience if they had any questions for Jim, Julie Matthews, the casting agent, asked, "I want to know why I didn't get paid extra for finding this guy... Jim's a jewel—not just an extra but a really good source for Bob to get stuff done." From the bottom of my heart, I'd like to say, "thank you," Mr. Schwartz and Ms. Matthews.

Casting *A Christmas Story*'s main characters came easy for Bob Clark.

He once said that he considered Jack Nicholson for the part of The Old Man but he had a limited budget and couldn't afford Jack. Darren had already worked in several other Bob Clark films, and they had a great working relationship, so Bob called Darren.

Darren McGavin had a very rough life. He and my brother Jim bonded over their shared experiences of growing up fast and working at a young age. Darren pursued his dream of acting and became a consummate actor. He really put his all into the "Old Man" character—gruff on the outside, but lovable and attentive to his family, nonetheless. Darren loved working with children and he didn't talk down to them. He was perfect for that role. When Darren was asked what he thought about *A Christmas Story*, he replied, "it will last."

The actress who portrayed Ralphie's mom, Melinda Dillon, was living in France at the time of *A Christmas Story* House opening day ceremony. She is a very prolific actress with an impressive past. She was nominated for an Academy Award for Best Supporting Actress as Jillian Guiler in *Close Encounters of the Third Kind*. She played a troubled woman named Teresa in *Absence of Malice* alongside the late great Paul Newman. One of the last films she made was in 2007, called *Reign Over Me*, and she was in three episodes of the television series *Heartland*, also in 2007. In his 2003 interview, Bob said he saw Melinda in *Close Encounters* and knew she was the actress for the role of Mrs. Parker.

Bob also explained in that same 2003 interview that he took one look at Peter's tape as "messy Marvin" in a Hershey's commercial and said, "he is Ralphie."

Later, Peter became a co-host of a show called *Real People*. This popular show had several co-hosts who would introduce real people, not actors, who had an unusual occupation or an unfamiliar hobby. He also had a small part as Tad in the movie *Paternity* with the late Burt Reynolds.

Peter Billingsley hasn't participated in the Cleveland activities with his old co-stars, but he is still active in the movies, preferring to work behind the scenes. He was a producer for the megahit *Ironman*. It's ironic that Peter has such a huge fan base, but stays out of the spotlight insofar as *A Christmas Story* is concerned. It's lucky for us that he continues to entertain moviegoers with great films in his adult life. I wonder if he still remembers my brother, "Mr. Jim."

Zack Ward (Skut Farkus) & Jim

Dwayne McLean as Black Bart

Jim, Tedde Moore (Miss Shields), & Dwayne McLean (Black Bart)

# My Brother Jim

When my brother Jim heard about Brian Jones' endeavor to open *A Christmas Story* House and Museum up to the public, he jumped right on the bandwagon. Jim was always a workaholic, sometimes working two jobs at a time. His opportunities in 1983 and 1993, working as Assistant Production Manager during the filming of *A Christmas Story* and *My Summer Story* was a dream for him. It also prepared him for his job thirteen years later.

Starting in 2006, Jim would walk about 50 feet from his front door and over to *A Christmas Story* Museum whenever he wanted, just to tell his stories about the making of that movie. How lucky can a guy get? He was over-the-top happy. He began working freelance in the Museum, coming and going as he pleased. His stories sent fans on a memorable trip of what it was really like back in 1983.

Jim had his pictures and memorabilia set up in the front room of the Museum, off the main path. That was a good thing because many times, especially during the holidays, people filled the entire room and stayed for as long as they liked, just to listen to him. Jim was an animated and very comical storyteller. Although he told those stories over and over for years, he always made them sound brand new, as if he was sharing his memories with you for the very first time. The fans were delighted. Jim was gifted that way. He just loved to make people happy. He never thought of it as work.

To quote Brian Jones, "it was best for both of us. Jim was quite the attraction for the Museum."

Although Jim captivated thousands of fans who visited *A Christmas Story* Museum over the years, there are still so many people who have never heard them before. When I told Jim that I was writing this book, he was so thrilled! When I'd talk about it with him, he was all smiles. Our dreams merged.

Jim lived in our childhood home for forty years, from 1976 until he passed away in October, 2016. Now Jim's son Michael lives in our childhood home. The Leg Lamp still stands in Jim's custom-made plexiglass display case that was installed in the attic window on the front of his house.  Driving by, you can see Jim's initials, "JM," on the front of the house, hung up under a blue dragon holding a huge white light ball. It's an eye-catcher.

When Jim stopped working at the museum, his pictures remained on the wall in the room where he spun his stories. His old co-workers would talk about his association with the movie, so Jim's memory was kept alive. Often, when we'd be out working in Jim's yard, fans passing the house would stop and ask about him if he wasn't outside with us.

One very hot Saturday in July, my husband Bob and I were working in Jim's front yard, just as we always did. Jim often sat outside "supervising" us, but on that sweltering day, he felt it was better if he stayed in his air-conditioned house. While I was raking, I heard a loud booming voice. I looked up to the left of me and saw a huge jeep-like truck driving down our street. There was no cover on the top. Around 25 people were sitting in about five rows of seats on top of the vehicle. The driver was also up there with them, speaking through a bullhorn. As they approached us, the driver bellowed out:

"On the right, ladies and gentlemen, is the home of Jim Moralevitz!"

I was dumbfounded.

Bob's back was to the street, so the driver stopped the truck and shouted out to Bob, "Are you Jim Moralevitz?" Bob turned around and said, "No," then went back to working in the yard. I shouted out to the driver that Bob was Jim's brother–in–law and I was Jim's sister. As soon as I said that, twenty-five cameras started clicking away at us.

I was shocked! I had been working in the hot sun for hours. I wore no makeup. My hair was a mess. My clothes were wet with sweat and sticking (I mean really sticking) to me. The very last thing I wanted or needed was to have my picture taken by all these tourists. I managed a weak smile while tightly holding onto the rake. I shudder to think of how many people still have that picture of me in their phones or cameras. Now I know what movie stars go through with paparazzi! The driver then continued down the street and said, "I'll tell you more about Jim Moralevitz in a little while, ladies and gentlemen." It was surreal.

I ran into the house and told Jim what happened with the driver and the tourists. I thought he would be as excited as I was. He looked at me and nonchalantly said, "Oh, that happens all the time."

I know the main reason they were clicking pictures wasn't just because we looked so glamorous, but because of Jim's inventive way of displaying his beloved Leg Lamp in the plexiglass garden box he had installed in his attic window specifically for his Leg Lamp. This particular lamp was a gift from Jim's friend and the owner of the House, Brian Jones. That made it all the more special. Jim kept the lamp lit twenty-four hours a day, seven days a week. Jim once said, "I will keep that Leg Lamp burning for as long as I live." He did.

Personally, I have mixed feelings about that famous Leg Lamp. I believe men love it more than women do, for some reason… The way the leg is cut off at the top and all the black fringe hanging down on a gold lampshade doesn't appeal to me. I know I'm in the minority about this because Brian Jones has had no problem selling them. A 2020 article written by Erika Wolf on mentalfloss.com reported that according to a post-Christmas press release that highlighted Amazon's seasonal sales in

Jim's Leg Lamp at night

Jim's Leg Lamp on display in the attic of his home

2012, the online retail giant boasted, "If you stacked every Christmas Story Leg Lamp purchased by Amazon customers that holiday season, the height would reach the top of Mt. Everest."

That "major award" Leg Lamp was modeled after an advertising logo for Nehi soda pop where a woman had a short skirt on and her legs were showing. Very brazen in 1942! In the logo, the nylons had a black seam going up the middle of the back of the leg. That was how nylons were sewn together back then. Also, that logo had two legs. The man responsible for manufacturing the very first Leg Lamp was Mr. Reuben Freed, who was Production Designer for the movie in 1983. As for the lampshade, according to Mr. Freed's 2009 interview in *Cleveland Magazine*, he thought of a lamp he had seen in his mother's house. It had a gold silk lampshade, pleated with fringe around it. He created a quick sketch of the lamp and showed it to Jean Shepherd, who approved it right away. According to Mr. Cassen Gaines, author of *A Christmas Story: Behind the Scenes of a Holiday Classic*, Mr. Freed produced three Leg Lamps for the movie, but they were broken during the filming of the movie. It was to be some type of "Lascivious Award that Heralded the Birth of Pop Art" for a Nehi contest that Mr. Parker entered.

The fact that Mr. Parker displayed it in the main living room window for all to see only added to its absurdity. While watching the movie, I really felt sorry for Mrs. Parker. I certainly would not want it in my front window, but many people do. I have seen it shining brightly in many homes and businesses during my trips across the country. Cleveland has its share, especially on the west side of the city, due in part because *A Christmas Story* House and Museum partners with local businesses in and around the Tremont area to display the lamp in their stores and restaurants.

Mementos from *A Christmas Story* were Jim's favorite gifts to hand out to our family every Christmas. When he saw how much I admired his inventive way of displaying the Leg Lamp in a plexiglass garden window attached to his house, he asked me if I wanted a Leg Lamp for my front window. I told him that I wasn't as crazy about it as he was and that I'll pass on that. I think he hoped that I would change my mind over time. As a result, I have a collection of Leg Lamp-themed items. I do not display them, but will forever treasure them in honor of Jim.

Less than two weeks before Jim died, there was one last unforgettable indication of his popularity. I was lucky enough to witness it.

It started out as our typical Saturday at Jim's. We expected to put in several hours of work in and around his house. Before work commenced, Jim mentioned that he wanted, and very much needed, a haircut. He asked Bob and me to take him to the nearby Steelyard Commons for a haircut.

Driving down the long road into the shopping complex, we were looking for a Best Cuts or a small barber shop. We didn't see any. Jim said to Bob, "Please drop me and Susie off in front of Walmart. I always get my hair cut there."

Walmart???

Bob and I glanced at each other, then he waited for me to help Jim get out of the car. We slowly walked into Walmart. At this time, Jim was very weak and took small steps. He spoke very softly and he was getting confused about little things.

Jim said, "let's go to the left, third door down." As we entered, we turned left, and when we arrived at the third door down, I found myself looking at a beauty salon that catered mostly to African-American women. All the beauticians were African-American women.

I said, "Jim, I don't think this is the right place."

He said, "Yes, it is—I come here all the time."

The beauticians stared at us as we entered, then continued to attend to their customers.

No one came up to the counter. There was one chair by the door.

I said to Jim, "Sit down, Hon, this might take a while."

We knew that Bob would be in the entertainment section at the back of the store, looking for cheap DVD movies. Jim said, "Sis, go on with Bob, I'll be ok." I hesitantly left him there. By the time Bob and I bought the movies and came back to the salon, Jim was seated in a styling chair. A very nice woman with friendly eyes was combing his long hair. I walked up to them. She couldn't make out Jim's mumbling, so she wasn't sure how to cut his hair. She asked me if I was his wife and if I knew what he wanted.

I said, "I'm not his wife, I'm his sister. Give him a Mohawk."

They both stared at me.

I laughed and said, "All he really needs is a trim, and to take a little off the top."

Jim said softly, "I come here all the time. Do what you did the last time."

She leaned over to look him in the face and finally recognized him.

She stood upright and shouted: "Oh my gosh, it's that mailman from that *Christmas Story* movie! Girls, get on over here, it's that mailman I told you about—from that Christmas movie! I cut his hair before!" They all gathered around him, laughing and talking about the movie.

Jim was grinning. I didn't correct her about the mailman comment—I was speechless at this turn of events. She cut his hair perfectly and even took the time to shave his beard. She didn't charge him extra for that. Jim thanked her and gave her a big tip.

There was a noticeable lightness to his step as we were walking out the door of Walmart. Jim felt good, and it showed. I will remember that day forever.

Jim had many articles written about him over the years, from major newspapers to an inquiry from a young writer who was doing a term paper about Jim.

Jim watched News Channel 5's noon news for years. His favorite television anchor was Leon Bibb. Jim was ecstatic when Leon asked to have an interview with him! Of course, Jim said "Yes!" It happened right in Jim's kitchen. Leon is quite a guy. I couldn't find the interview online, but I do have the picture of the two of them in Jim's kitchen.

Jim's favorite local newspaper reporter was Ms. Laura DeMarco, a columnist for the *Cleveland Plain Dealer*. She's written many articles about the House over the years. I especially liked her story about *A Christmas Story* House and Museum from December 5, 2013. It is a worthy read online. I loved the way Laura described her visit and how she captured Jim's essence in just a few paragraphs. There is one line she wrote that touches my heart: "The best part of the Museum isn't a what, it's a who: Jim Moralevitz."

It was because of that one line that Laura was the only newspaper reporter I contacted when Jim passed away. She replied with her condolences and mentioned him in her *Christmas Story* article on December 1, 2016.

I'm sure you've heard the saying, "opportunity knocks only once," or "you have to go searching for your destiny, it's not going to come to you." Well, Jim was the exception to these words of wisdom—three times.

The first time was when the trucks came rolling down the street and parked outside his house to unload the camera equipment needed to film *A Christmas Story*.

Leon Bibb & Jim

The second time opportunity knocked for Jim was in 1993, when Director Bob Clark once again brought Hollywood to W. 11th Street to film *My Summer Story*.

The third time was the charm: *A Christmas Story* House and Museum opened and Brian Jones encouraged Jim to work in the Museum as a storyteller.

The Museum became more than just a building of old artifacts—it came alive with Jim's stories. Many fans came to visit when the actors from the movie stopped by to sign autographs at *A Christmas Story* House and Museum, but the actors weren't there every day. They flew into Cleveland mostly around the holidays. Jim was there all the time—when his health allowed.

Sadly, Jim's career as a storyteller lasted around seven years. His throat cancer grew worse, even with chemo and radiation treatments. Here was a man who communicated for a living. Now he could no longer speak intelligibly. He was shattered by the disease and upset about not being able to work. Jim was in his 70s, but still not ready to retire. He really loved meeting people from all over the world and entertaining them. If it weren't for that cancer, I know in my heart that Jim would still be in that Museum up to this very day, doing what he loved, in that special way only he could do.

When Ian Petrella (Randy) came to Cleveland, he would stop and visit the House and Museum to sign autographs and pose for pictures with his many fans. He sometimes stayed overnight at *A Christmas Story* House, which made it easier to see the fans each day. Oh, they just love him. Jim was still working at the museum at that time and as a result, they resumed their friendship that started when the movie was filmed in 1983. Jim was so happy that "one of the boys" came home. Jim had his picture of Ian and Peter Billingsley drinking hot chocolate that Jim had made for them during a break between scenes, holding big blue mugs and sitting on the front porch of my childhood home.

One of my favorite quotes from my brother Jim: "Who'd a thunk it?" He wrote that quote along with his autograph on his Delivery Man photographs. On Christmas Day of 2009, Jim gave Leg Lamp ties to my three grandsons, Tyler, Zack, and Tom. The ties light up. The boys love them. Every Christmas, Jim would wear one of his many *Christmas Story* vests. He loved to wear vests, and he called these particular vests his "work uniforms." They all had *A Christmas Story* logo sewn on. I have one of them. He especially loved his black leather vest. He never went to work without wearing one of them. He wore a jacket with that logo also. On what would be his final Christmas Day in 2015, Jim came over to our house wearing his green *Christmas Story* pajama pants, saying that they were too comfortable to take off that morning.

I love my old neighborhood for all the memories of all the friends and relatives that I had there. There are only a handful now. When I visited Jim, fans would stop to take pictures of his Leg Lamp in the top window. If I was outside, they would stop and ask me about my memories of the filming of the movie and I would happily share them.

Many have asked me if the neighbors of *A Christmas Story* House and Museum were upset about the nonstop traffic and throngs of fans, especially during the holidays. Well, here's one neighbor's opinion: If anyone watched the passage of time on West 11th Street, it was our next-door neighbor, Mrs. Smele. She lived on that street long before I was born. Back in the day, especially before television, people sat on their front porch after dinner, and just talked. Among each other, face to face. Nearly every home had a radio, some had a television, but most people would keep the electronics off, go out into the cool evening air and just … talk. Mrs. Smele was on her front porch all the time. She started sitting out there with her mom, dad, and her husband. After they passed away and she was alone, Mrs. Smele still sat on her porch to talk with the neighbors. She started chatting with the fans of the movie as they parked down the street and passed her home walking to and from *A Christmas Story* House and Museum. She would happily recall her own memories of what it was like with all the movie stars mingling on her street. I wish I could have heard her stories before she left us. She passed away on April 5, 2008. She was a wonderful neighbor. She loved our family and truly loved how Jim made her laugh. He sat with her as often as he could. She spoiled him with her homemade meals and bakery. I did stop by to talk with Mrs. Smele back in 2007, but only for a short time. I asked her what she thought of all the traffic and commotion. Because of her age, I thought she would say something like: "It's too noisy," or "Too many crowds."—something of that nature. Instead, she sweetly said "Oh, I don't mind. The fans are very friendly." What a classy lady.

There are probably no more than a handful of people still living in that neighborhood who were around when the movie was being made. Most of them were extras. The new tenants living on those two surrounding blocks today have no idea how "quaint" the neighborhood was before *A Christmas Story* House and Museum existed. Back then, except for a few drunken brawls at Rowley Inn, it was very quiet. I remember running in and out of the streets to catch lightning bugs. We always played in the streets, because there really was very little traffic back then. Now, it's totally different. Throughout the year, the traffic never stops. There is always some kind of promotion going on. Even at night, when the House and Museum are closed, curious out-of-towners drive by.

I try to visit the House and Museum on a yearly basis, especially if Brian Jones is in town. On July 26, 2019, I went there for a yoga class in the backyard of the House! I am not kidding! On the way there, I texted Brian to ask if he would be there. His reply was that he wasn't in town and he didn't do yoga. Too bad, I would have loved to see that. I went with my friend, Lori Moore, and we had a great time. There were a handful of people and the weather was perfect. Afterwards, we had cookies and punch and were allowed access to the House and Museum for as long as we wanted! Although I am very familiar with the house, I had never been up to the third floor where the fans pay to stay the night. It's so bright and airy for an attic area. I was pleasantly surprised. It has a full-sized kitchen, comfortable furniture, several *A Christmas Story* games, and a TV with a DVD of the movie. I will plan an overnight trip sometime in the near future. I didn't expect to see all that when I signed up for the yoga class.

All in all, it was a great experience. Except for the dog poses, I would definitely do it again.

Jim with Jean Shepherd during the filming of *My Summer Story*. Jean co-wrote and narrated *A Christmas Story*.

Jim & Ian Petrella

Jim at *A Christmas Story House* and Museum

Jim's last Christmas, 2015

# Jim Went Home

*My original plan for this book has changed dramatically over the past few years. Life, and death, have a way of doing things like that. For over ten years, I've been writing this book from my memories about living near that famous house all my life and my recollections of watching the movie being filmed in Cleveland. Now I have added my brother Jim's stories to share with the many fans of* A Christmas Story.

I had no idea how heartbreaking and heartwarming this whole ordeal would become. At the end of his life, my little family visited Jim many times during his brief stay in the Malachi House center for the terminally ill. Two days before he died, Jim was still coherent. On that day, my husband Bob, my son Tim, my daughter-in-law Gia and my sister Dorothy were visiting with me. That was the day I made a deathbed promise to Jim. At that time, I didn't think of it as a deathbed promise. I really felt in my heart that he would start to eat more and get his strength back. I promised him that I would finally finish this book, with his photos included, and dedicate my book to him. I have fulfilled my promise.

I've written a lot about Jim in this book because his life became totally immersed with *A Christmas Story*. It started way back on the day that Julie the casting director walked into the Rowley Inn and asked who owned the house. Every time Jim came to our home for Thanksgiving and Christmas, he relayed stories to us about the hundreds of fans he met at *A Christmas Story* Museum. He just couldn't separate his personal life from his work. I have tried my best to share his stories with you.

Among his varied interests, photography was a big one. Jim just had a knack for picture-taking. He owned several expensive cameras.

Years ago, I told Jim that I had been writing a book about the house and neighborhood. The story I wanted to convey was what it was like before, during, and after the movie was filmed. I knew Jim had many personal pictures of Bob Clark and the actors, especially Darren McGavin. Because he was the chaperone for Peter and Ian, he took many endearing, natural pictures of the two of them. He loved to shoot from different angles and took a lot of pictures of the unsuspecting actors below when he was in the makeshift wardrobe department above the Rowley Inn.

Jim had hoped to one day make a coffee-table book of his pictures. After having done that, he said he would donate some of the pictures to the Museum. When cancer took over, he went through chemo treatments. He could barely talk. He knew he was not strong enough to undertake the large task of compiling a book of his photos and finding an editor and a publisher. He gave me all his beloved pictures and stacks of newspaper clippings that he cut out of various papers for over 30 years. Many of the newspapers were yellow and brittle with age.

He said, "Susie, take them. They're all yours." Jim didn't produce a book, but in 2008, he was able to participate in a documentary called *The Untold Christmas Story*. It boasts "Never Before Seen Photos and Interviews with the Cast Members!" Jim lent 25 copies of his "Never Before Seen Photos" to this film. In this documentary, Ian Petrella, Zack Ward, Scott Schwartz, Yano Anaya, and Tedde Moore share their fondest memories of their roles in the movie. Darren McGavin, Jean Shepherd and Bob Clark had all passed away by then.

Jim had a small part in this documentary. He reminisced about going to the Rowley Inn with his buddy Darren McGavin, and how Darren would call his wife to tell her that he's "having a cold one with my buddy, Jim." Jim mentioned in this film that they became close friends and that he missed Darren very much.

Another segment of the documentary has Jim in front of a map of North America. The map had dozens of colorful push pins in it, each representing visitors to the House from all over the U.S., Canada, and Mexico. Toward the end of the film, Brian Jones' dad mentioned how Jim made the Museum come alive by meeting and greeting the fans while telling them stories about filming *A Christmas Story.*

During the summer of 2016, Jim knew that he didn't have long to live. He told Bob and me that he didn't want a "big fuss" about him when he died. He didn't have to worry about us, because a lot of other people would make quite a fuss, and deservedly so.

Brian Jones and the staff at *A Christmas Story* House and Museum posted a wonderful tribute to Jim on their *Christmas Story House* Facebook page. A few of Jim's pictures were posted, including my favorite pic of "the buddies," Jim and Darren together. Many people posted their fond memories of listening to Jim tell his stories. Reading the comments touched my heart. Jim sure made a lot of people happy.

The day before Jim's memorial mass and luncheon, I stopped by the funeral home to pick up several things for his service. The very compassionate owner said to me, "I just read Jim's obituary. I had no idea that we had a local celebrity in our care." I told her to go online to *A Christmas Story* House Facebook page to read his tributes from people all over the country. Jim was pretty popular!

I miss him dearly, although I have felt his presence many times while writing this book. Deep in my heart I feel that he's proud of me.

# A Fra-GEE-lay Urn

Yes, there is such a thing.

Brian Jones had it custom made especially for Jim. It was his gift to our family. A gift that will be cherished forever.

It all came about when Jim's son Michael had planned to put Jim's cremains in *A Christmas Story* cookie jar that was shaped like *A Christmas Story* House. Michael called *A Christmas Story* Gift Shop to ask if they had a cookie jar in stock. Someone at the Gift Shop told Brian. Brian called and said he wanted to order a one-of-a-kind urn made just for Jim. It was in the shape of the Leg Lamp crate and had "FRAGILE' stamped on it. We were surprised and flattered. Brian was out of town, but had the urn delivered in time for Jim's memorial mass. It was perfect for Jim. I never asked Brian, but I believe this urn was one of a kind.

Jim's memorial mass and luncheon took place at St. Augustine's Church and Hall on November 5, 2016. That day marked the three-year wedding anniversary for my son Tim and his wife Gia. That day also marked the 100th anniversary of the birth of my dad. I'm sure our dad and mom were smiling down on us all.

We placed Jim's FRAGILE urn on a pedestal, next to a vase of carnations. It was up front, near the altar in church. It looked beautiful. Being a former altar boy, Jim got a kick out of this, I'm sure.

I always knew how much Jim loved everything that was associated with *A Christmas Story*, but it really hit me when I started going through his notes, fan letters and old yellowed newspaper articles that were shoved into bags and boxes. I had absolutely no idea how many lives he touched and how many people complimented him on just being … Jim.

I knew that thousands of people visited *A Christmas Story* House and Museum every year. What I didn't realize was how many of them posted their experiences on different internet websites! For example, on the TripAdvisor website alone, there were over 73 pages of reviews from visitors from around the world. Jim is favorably mentioned in several of them.

Here is a review from TripAdvisor that I treasure:

"A must see. The highlight of our trip."

5 of 5 stars, Reviewed June 6, 2010.

"This place was great! Any fan of the movie *A Christmas Story* has to come here. The employees are great and our tour guide (wish I could remember her name but she reminded us all of Kari on *Mythbusters*) was very good. She was great at suggesting re-enacting scenes for photos and was willing to take all the pictures of your family you could ask for. This is not a hands-off tour as you are allowed to roam the house, sit on the furniture and hide under the sink like Randy. The museum across the street is filled with photos and memorabilia from the movie (Wow! A zeppelin.). The gift shop offers everything from snuggies, to Monopoly, to candy and are all themed to the movie. We left with a load of Christmas presents for the family for this Christmas. Our highlight of the tour was meeting Jim Moralevitz, who was one of the freight men that delivered the "major award" crate. Jim was hired as an extra in the movie as were many of the other neighbors. Jim still lives in the house 2 doors down from Ralphie's and has some wonderful tales from his experiences with the movie, the director, and the stars. If you are ever in the Cleveland area you have to see this place if you don't do anything else."

Photo courtesy of Jennifer E. Skutnik

Photo courtesy of Barbara Crouse

An excerpt from a 2013 *USA Today* article:

Jim Moralevitz, now 73, lives down the street from *A Christmas Story* house and landed a cameo role in the film helping deliver the crate carrying the Leg Lamp.

The entrepreneur who developed the house as a tourist attraction, Brian Jones, gave Moralevitz a Leg Lamp seven years ago and it's mounted in a 6-foot outdoor Plexiglas box near the peak of the front roof. People sometimes mistake it for *A Christmas Story* house and stop to visit.

In the neighborhood, "I'm known for the most drive-by shootings (photos)," said Moralevitz, a retired tour guide stepping back into his old role for comic effect.

An article in the *Times of Northwest Indiana* on December 15, 2013:

CLEVELAND | South sider Jim Moralevitz thought he made it pretty big when his polka band, The Music Jesters, was making good money playing at weddings and bowling alleys.

Moralevitz would reach a much bigger audience.

Millions of people see him on television every Christmas because he offered the use of his driveway to a Hollywood cast and crew that swarmed over his working-man's neighborhood in south Cleveland three decades ago.

He got to work with Hammond native Jean Shepherd on the set of the beloved classic "*A Christmas Story.*"

"He's a wonderful man," Moralevitz said. "On set he mostly kept to himself and observed. He was arguing with (director) Bob Clark a few times."

Moralevitz lived a few homes down the street from the house where they filmed a movie — based on Shepherd's Hammond childhood — that is now shown for 24-hour-long marathons on cable television. Moralevitz helped get the production back on schedule by suggesting they ship in snow-making machines from a nearby Ohio ski lodge when it failed to snow, and appeared as an extra in one of the most memorable and oft-quoted scenes.

Moralevitz delivered the big wooden box marked fragile, which The Old Man pronounced "fra-GEE-lay" and said must be Italian. Inside was Old Man Parker's Major Award, a fishnet-stockinged Leg Lamp that has become an iconic symbol.

The crate was 6 feet tall and 4 feet wide, too big to fit through any doorway, so filming was stopped while union carpenters spent hours trimming 4 inches off the side with a handsaw. Careful viewers can spot their handiwork because the letters read "his side up," not "this side up." Moralevitz shares that anecdote with visitors from across the globe while guiding tours at the *A Christmas Story* House down the street.

The 73-year-old still lives down the block from the house where the movie was filmed, which was turned into a tourist attraction for smartphone picture-snapping parents in 2006. *A Christmas Story* House and Museum owner Brian Jones gave Moralevitz a Leg Lamp, which he proudly displays in his second-story window.

"At my age, I've lost so many friends, but I've gained so many friends to talk to through this movie," he said. "It gives me something to do, and I can walk two doors down. I will keep the Leg Lamp burning for as long as I live."

# Meeting Brian Jones

During the Christmas season in 2016, Bob and I wanted to meet with Brian Jones to thank him personally for his gift to our family. He went above and beyond in his tribute to Jim with the incredible "Fra-GEE-lay" urn. We also wanted to thank him for the very kind and moving tribute that was posted on *A Christmas Story* House Facebook page.

This was bittersweet for Bob and me. Although our nephew Michael lives in our family home, it's not the same as going there to visit Jim to help out around his house and unknowingly pose for pictures for movie fans. I will miss working in Jim's front yard and talking to the tourists about Jim and the movie.

Bob and I met Brian in *A Christmas Story* Gift Shop. When I saw all the Leg Lamps on display, I was overwhelmed. It was around two months after Jim's passing, just a few weeks before Christmas, and my emotions were still a bit raw. I started crying. Brian walked right up to us and gave me a hug. He conveyed how sad he was that Jim was gone. Brian also said that Jim was a good friend and that he loved having Jim work in the Museum, telling his "Jim stories." That was the beginning of our friendship.

When we walked in, I don't know why, but for some reason, we didn't expect to see Jim's photos, along with ours, still displayed on the wall. Our tears started falling. On display are sections of movie scripts that Jim donated, saved in a glass case. My Bob couldn't speak, he was so moved. Looking back, of course Brian would keep Jim's things as they were—they're part of the history of the movie! One thing I will never forget from that meeting with Brian was how much he appreciated knowing

Jim. Brian said that Jim was "the human connection to the movie, bridging the time gap between then and now with his recollections."

I sometimes find it hard to wrap my head around all the excitement these fans convey about *A Christmas Story* House and Museum because of my memories before the movie, when my friends and relatives lived ordinary lives in those ordinary houses. To get some idea, consider a few houses on your childhood street being transformed into a worldwide destination. It can be mind boggling!

I feel truly grateful that I was able to witness the filming of a few scenes in this wonderful movie. Back then, no one, certainly not me, had any idea what a phenomenon it would become. In 2012, *A Christmas Story* was selected by the Library of Congress for preservation in the National Film Registry as being "culturally, historically or aesthetically significant." It seems that this phenomenon will continue for a long, long time.

Back in 1969, our Cuyahoga River caught fire due to pollution and we were in the worldwide spotlight. The upside was that this incident heightened public awareness and helped form the Environmental Protection Agency (EPA) in 1970. The downside, of course, was that Cleveland became identified with this environmental disaster.

Brian Jones & me

Brian and Beverly Jones' investment in what is now a complex of four buildings dedicated to *A Christmas Story* has contributed to putting the city of Cleveland in the worldwide spotlight once again. But this time it's for only positive reasons—not because of a burning river, but because of a burning bulb—in a Leg Lamp—in a House.

Brian Jones & me

# Epilogue

Well, dear readers, that's my story.

What's yours?

As I stated earlier in the book, we all have our own Christmas Story "story." Here's your chance to bring your memories to life and be a part of *A Christmas Story* history!

Describe your story in 500 words or less and e-mail me at: mychristmasstory83@gmail.com.

A selection of the essays received will be compiled in my newest book and will include only your first name, city, and state.

The deadline for entry and the date of publishing will be determined by the total number of essays received, which will be announced via My Christmas Story 'story' Facebook page at a later date.

If you have a short comment about your own experience with *A Christmas Story,* or if you want to share what you liked most about this book, please post it on My Christmas Story 'story' Facebook page. I look forward to hearing from you.

Happy Writing!

S.S.

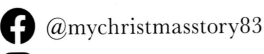

@mychristmasstory83

@mychristmasstory83

# Acknowledgements

This book is my gift to you. The following friends and coworkers have given me their gifts of love, time, and devotion. They helped me make my dream a reality.

I have to start with the late great Becky Almodovar, who believed in me from the very beginning and gently but firmly persuaded me to believe in myself. I miss her every single day.

I am so grateful for my dear friend and first editor, Brian Jones, who encouraged me to just "go for it." His enthusiasm for all things related to *A Christmas Story* is a joy to see. He is always just a text away and knowing I can count on him makes my life so much easier.

I cannot forget my adopted-by-love sisters, because they are unforgettable—Alice, Barb, Barbara, Diane, Ellie Mae, Georgeann, Jen, Judy, Julie, Kim, Lisa, Natalie, and Vivian. No last names are needed. They know. These sisters helped me through the rough times and cheered me on for the last several miles of this journey, right up to the finish line.

Two of my childhood friends are still a part of my life, Chris Moralevitz and Helen Ivanov. They have shown me unconditional love and support through our many years together and I know they will be my friends to the end. The warm, happy, safe, and enjoyable years of my youth are mostly due to my surroundings of the friends and families I have known and loved in my little neighborhood. They are too numerous to mention. Many of them have passed away, but their memories will always live in my heart.

I believe in fate. God puts us exactly where we need to be, when we need to be there. Just at the right time, many unexpected doors have opened for me. I am fortunate to have a kind and understanding doctor, Jennifer Snyder, M.D. She's the best caretaker and graciously introduced me to her very talented daughter, Jordan Laird, who became my valued and proficient second editor.

I owe many thanks to my dear buddy Connie, aka Luke, who is my inspiration for tenacity with grace. Connie introduced me to her son, James Renner, a very clever and visionary author. He has quite a busy life but always takes the time to help me and has given me valuable advice. Thanks to James, I have found the kindest and most patient attorney, David P. Thomas, Esq.

One of the highlights of this journey was when I connected with Sunny Day Publishing, LLC. My wonderful publishers, Dr. Pam Connery (Levinson) and Stacie Hancher Gerrity, have held my hand and walked me through every step of this incredible experience. They are true professionals. My patient final editor, Ruth Beach, whose skillful advice was invaluable to me.

I thank God every day for my loving family. My life is far from boring, thanks to my son Tim and daughter-in-law Najeah, whose encouragement and support I will always cherish. My daughter Carol, son-in-law Mark, and my three incredible grandsons, Tyler, Zackery and Thomas Kis. I saved the best for last, my husband Bob, whose incredible love and faith are without end.

I love you all.

Made in the USA
Monee, IL
24 October 2023

44814705R00067